INSPIRATIONAL HOMES IN STUNNING LOCATIONS

GREAT ESCAPES

JUDITH MILLER WITH PHOTOGRAPHY BY **SIMON UPTON**

RYLAND
PETERS
& SMALL

LONDON NEW YORK

First published in the United States in 2000
by Ryland Peters & Small, Inc.
519 Broadway, 5th Floor
New York, NY 10012
www.rylandpeters.com

Text copyright © Judith Miller 1999, 2000
Design and photographs copyright
© Ryland Peters & Small 1999

10 9 8 7 6 5 4 3

ISBN 1-84172-106-9

A CIP catalog record for this book is
available from the Library of Congress.

Printed in China

Senior Designer Paul Tilby
Editor Hilary Mandleberg
Editorial Assistants Tessa Thornley,
                          Miriam Hyslop
Location Research Manager Kate Brunt
Location Assistant Sarah Hepworth
Production Director Meryl Silbert
Art Director Gabriella Le Grazie
Publishing Director Anne Ryland

Contributors Eithne Power, Lynn Bryan

CONTENTS

FOREWORD

Escape has meant different things to me at various stages of my life. You might think that when I was growing up in the Borders of Scotland, surrounded by gentle rolling hills and wonderful views of the River Tweed, the desire to escape would have been the farthest thing from my mind. But far from it: as a young teenager in the 1960s, the glamour of life in the city was one of my ultimate goals. And so I left, to experience it, for four years, while at university in Edinburgh.

After this, escape of a different sort beckoned—in the form of a spell working on a remote sheep station in Mackenzie country, on the Canterbury plains of New Zealand's South Island. Returning to Britain, I spent many years in Kent—the "garden of England"—before my work drew me to the metropolis. Having lived in London for some six years now, I often find myself longing once again for the wide open spaces.

But where would I escape to now . . . and what would I live in? Would I sensitively restore an ancient cottage, such as the Crooked House in Wales, or design the strikingly up-to-date perfect modern retreat, like the spiritual dwelling in Tepotzlán, Mexico, or the high-tech minimalist Topanga Canyon home in California? Or perhaps I'd feel the lure of a traditionally designed group of *palapas* on the west coast of Mexico, where the jungle meets the Pacific Ocean. Would I opt for the totally different lifestyle offered by the water tower near Antwerp in Belgium, or the early-twentieth-century Great Camp escape in the beautiful Adirondacks? Or maybe I'd go "back to nature" in the Guest Tent in the Pennsylvania woods around the Delaware River.

In addition to coping with scorpions and snakes in Mexico, and fleeing from a magnificent black bear on the banks of the Delaware, researching this book has allowed me to investigate these and many other escapes. As you will see, I have been lucky enough to discover some glorious locations—some truly Great Escapes. Each posesses different attractions and fulfills different needs, but each has some very special allure. I suspect you will find, as I did, that you could be quite happy living in almost any of them.

INTRODUCTION

This book is a celebration of escape—the desire to get away from the mundane realities of everyday life and from its stresses and strains. That desire is common to virtually all cultures and historical periods, but, until comparatively recently, the ability to achieve it was largely confined to the ruling classes and the super-rich. Today, escape is a real possibility—and because of the demands that modern life makes on us, a necessity—for the masses, too. A whole new leisure industry has blossomed in the second half of the twentieth century. The result is that many of us now spend a lot of our time and money trying to "escape."

The escape can take many forms. It may be nothing more than an evening in front of the television, enjoying a night out with friends, or spending a vacation doing nothing much on a sunny beach, or it may be a more active type of escape—a hiking or bicycling holiday, a weekend gardening, a workout at the gym. Then there are those of us who seek a more permanent type of escape, something that brings a greater sense of fulfillment or a more satisfying spiritual life. We may look for this through religion, yoga, or meditation, or we may find it by returning to our primeval roots in the countryside, by seas and lakes, in mountains and on hillsides, or in woodlands—those places where people lived before the march of progress lured many of us to what appeared to be a better life in the towns and cities.

Looking back in time, one can see how this complex modern concept of escape has developed. The ruling classes in ancient Persia, for example, believed that stimulation of the senses was essential for the rejuvenation of body, mind, and spirit, so they constructed *parridaeza* (the origin of our word paradise)—oases of water surrounded by beautiful gardens filled with herbs and aromatic shrubs and flowers. Here they could wander, relax, and escape from the onerous tasks of government.

Meanwhile, the ancient Greeks developed a philosophy of providing for the needs of the "whole man." Aware of the stresses and strains of political and military life, they often built villas and gymnasiums around sites of religious significance so that civic dignitaries could worship, debate matters of philosophy and state, and exercise in tranquility and comfort.

With the spread of the Greek empire under Alexander the Great, this philosophy was widely disseminated all over the Mediterranean and beyond. It was enthusiastically adopted by the Romans. In the first century B.C., the influential Roman architect, historian, and commentator Vitruvius wrote extensively about Hellenistic pleasure gardens, and of villas being specially positioned in order to maximize the enjoyment of the natural beauty of the site and the surrounding countryside. Wealthy, influential Romans followed this example, none more memorably than Emperor Hadrian in the second

century A.D. To achieve some respite from the machinations of governing a rapidly expanding empire and, particularly, from the constant intrigues of the Roman Senate, he commissioned a superbly luxurious villa on a man-made marble island—the Maritime Island—that could only be reached via two wooden swing bridges.

With the spread of Christianity in Europe came a greater emphasis on escaping the sins of the flesh and on seeking spiritual enlightenment. Religion (and superstition) played a large part in the lives of everybody, rich and poor. Cathedrals and churches were built throughout Europe, and with them came places of pilgrimage, monasteries, and nunneries. Even the most ordinary people could escape from the everyday hardship of their working lives, either temporarily, by attending church services where they could briefly be transported by the ceremonial to a world of bliss and salvation, or permanently, by becoming members of one of the many religious orders. In the bosom of such orders, presumably, bliss and salvation were rather more long-lasting.

Moving on through history to the mid-eighteenth century, increasing commercial activity

YOU DO NOT NEED TO LEAVE YOUR ROOM ... REMAIN ... AT YOUR TABLE AND LISTEN. DO NOT EVEN LISTEN, SIMPLY WAIT. DO NOT EVEN WAIT, BE QUITE STILL AND SOLITARY. THE WORLD WILL FREELY OFFER ITSELF TO YOU

and new scientific developments fueled the early stages of the Industrial Revolution. As a result, this period saw a substantial migration from the countryside, and a huge growth in the size and influence of cities and towns. But, in the latter part of the century came the reaction. What people now needed, so it was said, was to turn their backs on urban life and go "back to nature." This rural romanticism was given additional credence by Jean-Jacques Rousseau, the influential

French philosopher, who propounded the belief that human beings are essentially good but are corrupted by urbanization and civilization. Needless to say, such philosophizing was the province of the wealthy classes—the aristocracy and the landowners. The rest of society had no choice but to live as best they could in town or country—wherever chance had planted them at birth.

For the wealthy, the rural revival showed itself in a number of ways, but in the homes of such people the most obvious manifestations were a fascination with a more natural style of landscape gardening—the name of the English garden designer "Capability" Brown springs to mind—the construction of quaint architectural follies and grottoes in the grounds of their houses, and the elevation of the country cottage in people's minds to the status of a desirable dwelling.

This latter is best exemplified, and also best caricatured, by the story of the French queen Marie Antoinette who, in 1783, to "escape" from the formalities and constraints of the court of Versailles, the grandest palace in Europe, comissioned Louis XVI's court architect, Richard Mique, to design Le Hameau (The Hamlet). A group of quaint, rustic, half-timbered and thatched cottages at one end of the park of Versailles, they offered her and her closest friends a world of pastoral simplicity.

However, all was not quite as it seemed. No ordinary peasant or commoner could have lived in such a place for, in their decoration, Marie Antoinette's apartments in Le Hameau were a mirror-image of the grandeur of the court she was purporting to reject. The furniture, for instance, far from being rustic, was made by two of the greatest French *ébénistes* of the eighteenth century, Jean-Henri Reisener and Georges Jacob.

Despite this anomaly, Marie Antoinette took her "escape" with extreme seriousness. Wearing a light muslin "peasant" dress (which scandalized the court), she watched her strawberries being picked, visited her favorite (perfumed)

ABOVE **Sitting under a canopy at a Great Escape in Malibu, California, one cannot but be captivated by the sight and sound of the Pacific Ocean as its waves break on the sands. The view is so magical that the owner has designed the house with a huge floor-to-ceiling window so it can be enjoyed from inside as well as out.**

cows, and drank their milk from a jug made from the finest Sèvres porcelain.

As is well known, the French Revolution swept all this away and shook Europe to its core in the process. A new world order was to follow. While, at the end of the eighteenth century, the desire—and the ability—to escape from city life or simply from the stresses and strains of normal hard work was generally confined to a social, political, and economic élite, during the course

of the nineteenth century, it spread to a much larger section of the western world's rapidly expanding population—the newly affluent middle classes. For, as well as an increase in international trade, one of the major benefits of the Industrial Revolution was a more widespread distribution of wealth and the rise of this class of people.

The downside, however, was considerable. The overcrowding of, and the pollution, stench, and accompanying diseases prevalent in, many cities—the latter caused by a proliferation of factories, the burning of fossil fuels, and either totally inadequate or barely efficient sewerage systems—became close to intolerable. For the greater numbers who could now afford it, the restorative powers of the countryside, seaside, and even overseas travel, beckoned as never before. Moreover, substantial improvements to the infrastructure—especially the railroads, but also the roads—made getting away from it all far more feasible. For the first time "escape" was a thing to which the masses could aspire.

In Europe, one consequence of these developments was a substantial rise in the popularity of many spa towns, most notably Baden-Baden in Germany, and Tunbridge Wells and Bath in England. In some cases, such as at Lourdes, in France, the attraction of the baths was redoubled by the possibility of visitors benefiting from divine intervention and enjoying a miraculous recovery from an otherwise incurable disease.

Equally significant in Europe was the growing enthusiasm of the middle classes for the seaside. Here they could enjoy the restorative air and the invigorating water. Brighton, on the south coast of England, became fashionable at the beginning of the nineteenth century, in no small part thanks to the patronage of the Prince Regent (later George IV), and his commissioning (and part-designing) of that most extravagant of "escape homes," the Orient-inspired Brighton Pavilion.

On the opposite side of the Atlantic, greater prosperity gave added impetus to the building of

many substantial houses in the manner of that European prototype—the country estate. Particularly noteworthy examples include Monticello, the country house of Thomas Jefferson, remodeled at the turn of the nineteenth century in a blend of then-fashionable Palladian architecture and neoclassical decorations and furnishings, and the Italianate-style home of General Ulysses S. Grant, designed in about 1860.

However, such houses were not confined to ex-presidents of the United States. Many affluent New York merchants invested in palatial, neoclassical Federal and Empire-style houses in the Hudson River Valley, while in the southern states, landowners with plantations in Louisiana built equally prestigious homes on the other side of the Mississippi, in Natchez—where they could not only enjoy a better social life, but could also avoid the malaria and other diseases associated with the Louisiana swamps.

In many respects, the late nineteenth and early twentieth centuries provide some of the most compelling evidence of the human desire to keep in touch with, or to re-establish that fundamental link with nature that had been propounded in an earlier age by Jean-Jacques Rousseau and his ilk.

As far as the United States was concerned, this was a period of unprecedented urban development and economic growth, in which many prospered, but none more than the industrialists of New York. Families such as the Carnegies and the Vanderbilts, who had amassed vast fortunes from boom industries such as steel, lumber, and the railroads, may have lived in the lap of luxury in their urban mansions, but still felt the need to escape the city environs.

This was something they achieved from the late 1880s on by commissioning influential architects such as William West Durant to design a series of log-built lodges in the forests and mountains of the Adirondacks. Known as the Great Camps, these rustic retreats drew their architectural inspiration from the log cabins of the early American pioneers, such as Davy Crockett, James Fenimore Cooper, and Daniel Boone, from the lumber and mining camps of the

LEFT AND RIGHT In every culture, religious buildings attract the weary heart and the sickened soul. Many are on the site of earlier holy places, not necessarily of the same religion. This 16th–17th-century Christian seminary and convent, with its cloistered courtyard, stands in the small village of Tepoztlán in Mexico. Surrounded by volcanic mountains, the valley has long been regarded by the native Mexican Indians as a place of healing. The convent is overlooked by the three ancient pyramids of Tepoztlán, Malinalco, and Xochicalco— a permanent reminder of the valley's pre-Christian history.

LIVE WITH THE GODS. AND HE DOES SO WHO CONSTANTLY SHOWS THEM THAT HIS SOUL IS SATISFIED WITH WHAT IS ASSIGNED TO HIM

eighteenth and nineteenth centuries in the Adirondacks themselves, and from the log chalets of the European Alps. Moreover, the camps of the Adirondacks, in their turn, inspired the construction of many similar retreats in the forests of the northern-tier states along the Canadian–United States border, as well as in the south and west of the United States.

Despite the fact that these very grand lodges were, unlike the far more rudimentary frontier housing upon which they were based, architect-designed, extremely expensive and, rather like Marie Antoinette's Hamlet, playthings of the rich, their real significance resided in the way in which they tapped into the American psyche and its inextricable relationship with the frontier spirit and the call of the wild. Indeed, this desire to return to a simpler, more self-sufficent, and

WHEN FROM OUR BETTER SELVES WE HAVE TOO LONG BEEN PARTED BY THE HURRYING WORLD, AND DROOP, SICK OF ITS BUSINESS, OF ITS PLEASURES TIRED, HOW GRACIOUS, HOW BENIGN IS SOLITUDE

somehow more honest lifestyle—albeit the hunting, shooting, and fishing only took place at weekends and at vacation time—was to become, during the course of the twentieth century, not just the preserve of the American super-rich. For example, during the Great Depression of the 1930s, the administration of President Roosevelt took on thousands of out-of-work laborers whose job it was to build a series of rather more simply constructed log lodges in the National Parks—Glacier and Yellowstone, for example. Here, ordinary American citizens could come, at reasonable cost, to enjoy their natural heritage and find respite from their everyday urban existence.

This democratization of what could perhaps best be described as a conscious back-to-nature

movement, or search for an "escape," was one of the hallmarks of the twentieth century. It was given added impetus by the gradual provision during that century of better working conditions, which, in most parts of the developed world, have allowed workers to benefit from regular, annual paid vacations. Inevitably, given the diversity of human aspirations, the "great escape" that people have sought during these vacation periods has taken many different forms.

In the spirit of the early nineteenth century, one of the most attractive and most accessible holiday escapes for many people has undoubtedly been the seaside. However, with the advent of cheap air travel and the late-twentieth-century cult (and status) of the sun tan, the preferred seaside destination for large numbers of dwellers in the northern hemisphere has usually been one in sunny overseas climes—the Gulf or the Mediterranean. As a result, many of the old-established beach resorts, whose popularity once resided in such attributes as their bracing sea air, have seen a decline in their popularity.

Similarly, the idyll of the country cottage, built in the vernacular tradition and surrounded by a cultivated yet "wild" garden—echoes of Jean-Jacques Rousseau again—has once again become a weekend and/or retirement goal for numerous city dwellers, notably in Europe.

ABOVE AND RIGHT **It is still possible in the Adirondacks in northern New York state to experience the rich natural beauty that made the late-nineteenth and early twentieth-century industrialists build their summer camps there.** OPPOSITE **Hawkstone Park, Shropshire, England, was built in "rural romantic" style by Sir Rowland Hill in the eighteenth century. It comprises caves, cliffs, and this picturesque folly.**

For those on both sides of the Atlantic, with something of the pioneering spirit about them, mountains, lakes, forests, and even deserts and arctic wastes, beckon. These are people who are drawn to the ski chalets of Austria and Switzerland, to the hunting lodges of Germany and Russia, to the wood-built cabins in forests alongside the lakes of Canada or Sweden, to trekking in the foothills of the Himalayas and sleeping under canvas, to the adobe dwellings of Mexico and Santa Fe, or to the converted crofts and castles of Scotland. All these locations and many others have come to exert a powerful hold on the human imagination, for each offers the possibility of temporary or permanent escape

BUILDING UPON THE LAND IS AS NATURAL TO MAN AS TO OTHER ANIMALS, BIRDS, OR INSECTS

from the endless rat-race of overcrowded, over-stressed late-twentieth-century metropolitan life.

A large part of the attraction of such escapes undoubtedly lies in their natural physical environment. This can be calming or enervating, depending on what an individual feels he or she needs for their physical, mental, and spiritual rejuvenation.

neoclassical, Federal, and Empire mansions of the Hudson River Valley. The late eighteenth and early nineteenth centuries also saw a revival of the gothic style, originally the product of an age when, as perceived by people living three hundred years later, life was simpler and therefore more perfect. Similarly, in the United States, the late nineteenth century saw an upsurge in the popularity of Colonial-Georgian architecture, resulting in the building of many Colonial-Revival houses, while in Britain, the Arts and Crafts movement, led by William Morris, called for a renewed interest in English vernacular building—the sort of architecture that appears to have grown organically out of the countryside in response to the needs of country living—and a reaction against everything mass-produced.

**LEFT AND OPPOSITE
The Samuel-Novarro
House in Los Angeles was
built in 1926 by Frank
Lloyd Wright's eldest son,
also Frank. A massed
concrete and stucco block
rising dramatically from
the street forms the
essence of this urban
escape. The walled garden
adds to the secluded feel.
BELOW Many escapees
prefer native architecture.
Here a palm roof shades
the view of the Pacific near
Sayulita in Mexico.**

One reason for the popularity of all these historical-revival styles was that they recalled a bygone and, supposedly, better age—and in that sense they are very much part of the history of "escape." Nevertheless, whether contemporary, historical, or even futuristic, the most successful "escape" homes are usually those in which both the materials and the style of architecture and ornament have been harmoniously integrated with their natural surroundings. For, at the end of the day, it is Nature that provides the locations for escape, but it is up to the architects, designers, and owners to summon up the imagination to exploit these locations in a sympathetic manner.

However, as history shows, the architecture of the escape also plays a crucial role in that process. In many cases, the style of building and decoration has been decided by what is currently in vogue and that, in turn, has often been some sort of historical-revival style. For example, Greek and Roman villas have regularly been perceived as the model to which people should aspire. The High-Renaissance villas of fifteenth-century Tuscany harked back to such examples, as did the late eighteenth and early nineteenth-century

RURAL ESCAPES

Leaving the city for the countryside, be it for the weekend or for the length of a complete lifetime, is a conscious, deliberate act. Yet perhaps it is the subconscious that drives us there, that subliminal connection with the rhythm of nature and the changing flow of the seasons that those of us who live and work in the city do not realize we have, but that has been part of the human psyche since time began.

Nowhere is that connection more keenly felt than in a rural setting, where feeding, nurturing, and respecting the earth so that it provides for our needs, and having to follow nature's endless cycle rather than the demands of lesser forces brings with it a gentler, more compassionate, and more humane way of life.

The owners of the homes featured here have all aspired to, and have found, that gentler way of life. They have sought release from the mad, hectic, fast-paced round of city living and have discovered instead the beauty of nature's rhythm. Perhaps it is this

that makes their hearts beat a little faster as they turn the last bend on the long and winding road to their rural escapes.

The unadorned Moroccan farmhouse and the pair of old cottages—one set in the heart of the Welsh countryside, the other in the English—are simple structures at heart, not complicated by any architectural trickery or special effects. For who needs special effects when the surrounding countryside is imbued with so many natural wonders, be they a lush, flourishing date-palm oasis with a distant view of the brooding Atlas Mountains, an idyllic lake encircled by a glade of ancient oak trees, with winding streams and woodland walks, or the rolling Welsh hills dotted with grazing sheep and wooded valleys?

Each of these rural homes is the result of a magical combination—the mingling of an old, existing building imbued with the "spirit of place" and an owner's private dreams and imaginings. Looking to the past, finding out what worked for the original inhabitants, observing a year's natural cycle, noting the change of seasons and the effect of the modulating light at different times of the year is what has given each of the present owners an understanding of and a respect for that spirit of place, a sense of its continuity. For even though the rural building may now only be a weekend retreat, it is imperative that it retain its sense of solid permanence and its long-time connection with the earth. That is what makes it peaceful and harmonious. That is what envelops one, and that is what makes the perfect rural escape.

A tumbledown haven of peace in the rolling Welsh hills, the Crooked House glories in its age and unique vernacular architecture.

THE CROOKED HOUSE

The Crooked House in the Welsh mountains lies at the end of a short rough and ready track. On this picturesque adventure, the traveler looks out over a wooded valley through which a tributary of the River Lugg gently meanders. It's just about here that Herefordshire meets mid-Wales.

Then at last there is the Crooked House, where a sixteenth-century cruck-framed building merges with a "two-up-two-down" seventeenth-century wood-framed cottage and an eighteenth-century barn in fine Celtic harmony. With its roof that's a wild switchback of two-tone tiles and corrugated iron, the Crooked House could have come straight from a fairy tale by Hans Christian Anderson. For the couple who bought it, it was what they had searched for long and hard.

Their philosophy is a simple one, formulated with the help of some searching questions. Why pillage an old house just because you've become

its owner? Why not just let it be, let it stay in the shape it has taken over time? Why impoverish vernacular architecture in the name of restoration? What, they ask, is restoration all about? Can one not adapt one's needs to the building? Surely, having stood this long, with its crooked windows, crazy roof, and a list to starboard, the Crooked House must know best?

The Crooked House, now painted with a mix of whitewash and pigment known locally as raddle, has been settling into its foundations since the seventeenth century, and perhaps earlier. Linked-up farm buildings of this type are a vernacular tradition under constant threat from gentrification. In New England, constructions like these were immortalized in a children's song: "Big house, little house, back house, barn."

THE VERNACULAR HOUSING STOCK OF WALES IS BEING IMPOVERISHED IN THE NAME OF RESTORATION. I BELIEVE IN BUILDINGS RETAINING THEIR TIME-WORN SHAPE

THE VERNACULAR HOUSING STOCK OF WALES IS BEING IMPOVERISHED IN THE NAME OF RESTORATION. I BELIEVE IN BUILDINGS RETAINING THEIR TIME-WORN SHAPE

THE CHARM, ATTRACTION, CHARACTER, CALL IT WHAT YOU WILL, OF THE HOUSE IS THAT IT HAS GROWN OVER THE YEARS IN A HAPHAZARD SORT OF WAY

So, in flight from the present century, with its fixtures and fittings, stresses and conformities, the owners have welcomed the Crooked House's old-age cracks, eccentric character, and wonky lines. When they bought the house twenty-odd years ago, sheep and a handful of cows were gently grazing within its derelict walls, there was no water or electricity, and daylight was visible through the many cracks and gaping holes in the roof. But they were undeterred.

Now, twenty years later, with constant work but no professional help apart from with the plumbing, with the installation of some structural beams, and with the introduction of limited electricity, they can look out on the gentle hills all around, and say they've achieved what they wanted.

With their desire to preserve rather than rebuild, they have retained the flagstoned eighteenth-century kitchen, which stands in the wood-framed

cottage part of the house. This kitchen is dominated by a huge fireplace with a spit-rack, a pivoting sway for holding cooking utensils, and, high above the fire, a smoking rack that sits in its original slots. A door leads to the parlor—we are still in the wood-framed part of the house—with some original wattle-and-daub wall panels and whitewashed walls and ceiling.

Next door to these two rooms, in the part of the Crooked House that contains the oldest piece of lumber—a cruck beam, smoke-blackened from the open, central hearth that once burned here—stands a nineteenth-century kitchen, complete with restored bread oven and working cast-iron range. And, if that weren't enough, next to the nineteenth-century kitchen is the twentieth-century kitchen, where the refrigerator is clad in elm planks, a range oven cooks meals for paying guests and heats the water, and where the "sink" consists of a six-

GREAT ESCAPES

office

MCC

SPC

Don't remove from

OPPOSITE **In the wood-framed part of the Crooked House, flaking whitewash tinted with natural pigment covers original wattle-filled walls, oak beams, and doors just as it would have in the seventeenth century.**
LEFT **The main parlor in the seventeenth-century cottage boasts a comfortable mix of seventeenth- and eighteenth-century oak and fruitwood furniture. Although well researched to maintain authenticity, nothing in the Crooked House feels contrived. Everything is in regular use, from the open fire to the bread oven, to the earthenware pots and woven baskets—even the rush-light holder on the parlor table. The tiny window in one wall would have been designed with a view to keeping the parlor cool in summer and warm in winter.**

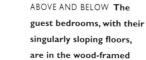

foot- (two-meter-) long slate milkcooler.

Although the original cruck-framed building would have been a single-story construction, the Crooked House now boasts two and, in places, three, storys, reached by five staircases—six if you include the ladder leading from one of the guest bedrooms to the attic above, and the drawbridge from the second floor to the yard.

On the second floor, in addition to a bathroom, are three bedrooms with feather beds, one of which is a fine four-poster. Duck under the cruck in the master bedroom, and you reach the Red Sitting Room, which stands above the dairy, the two forming a wing added in 1984.

Work on the Crooked House is hard and neverending, but it is a labor of love. The result is a unique, welcoming home that bears its age proudly, boasting to the world of its survival.

ABOVE AND BELOW **The guest bedrooms, with their singularly sloping floors, are in the wood-framed part of the house. Here, sections of the original wall construction are on view. The beds have feather mattresses placed on taut ropes, hence the saying "sleep tight." To get a firm mattress and hence a good night's sleep, you had to tighten the wooden pegs holding the ropes.**

MOROCCAN CHIAROSCURO

Hidden behind ancient mud walls, this extended farmhouse is surrounded by lush vegetation and water gardens—an oasis of delight in the desert.

This is a retreat that is best reached by night. To relish its true nature, leave Marrakesh behind and drive along a road that verges on the edge of the Atlas Mountains until the black top peters out and there is nothing but the pitch-black night and the stars. Suddenly you will stumble upon the old wooden gates of a farmhouse completely surrounded by ancient, mysterious mud walls. They conceal a green oasis flourishing with dates, olives, bougainvillaea, bananas, and rosemary. A winding path takes you to the door.

The farmhouse, a monument to old methods of building with straw and mud bricks, is at the heart of a five-acre (two-hectare) farm. The area, known as the Palmeraie, or date-palm oasis, once extended as far as Marrakesh.

The architect-owner, one of the foremost architects in Morocco, has built on adobe additions with Moroccan details to what is essentially a simple agricultural building. Once apprenticed to the distinguished Moroccan architect Charles Boccara, he also studied in Paris where he was inspired by the Egyptian architect Hassan Fathy. In the Egypt of the 1940s, Fathy succeeded in reviving the art of building with mud. By the

Although it is at the edge of the desert, the garden enjoys heavy rainfall, so it grows prolifically. It was mature in just two years, and after five, severe cutting back was needed. An olive grove in the 1940s, it now boasts a huge variety of plants many of which started life as cuttings given by friends, as seeds collected during travels, or salvaged from garbage dumps. The most successful are the cacti grown from cuttings from Yves Saint-Laurent's garden.

Wishing to add a grand salon to a structure that had started life as a simple agricultural building, the owner used traditional materials and recycled architectural details. The resulting mix of nineteenth-century cedar shutters, eucalyptus and oleander-reed ceiling, terracotta pigments, lacy metalwork grilles over unglazed windows, and elaborate eighteenth-century-style fanlights brings an organic feel to the design. The overall impression is one of comfortable grandeur where the seemingly unconscious juxtaposition of old and new furnishings and ceramics creates a cornucopia of amazing textural effects.

1980s, when its present owner bought the property in a ruinous condition, mud-based building had been abandoned in Marrakesh, but, in this earth-scorched terrain, mud seemed the natural choice. The only problem was finding the craftsmen to carry out the work, but it was a challenge that the owner pursued with his customary energy and his inherent criticism of modernity.

The result of all his work is a stunning three-bedroom, single-story house. The old part has become a pair of guest rooms opening onto a delightful sitting area. This has bench seating with comfortable, fat cushions and elegant, old, painted, arched wooden screens on two sides. The guest rooms share a bathroom that is nothing more than a shower and primitive toilet.

The new, L-shaped mud-brick extension wraps itself around a shady inner courtyard and is linked to the old part by a strange assemblage of kitchens, one without a roof and the other with. In the extension are found the master bed-

IN VIOLENT AND CHAOTIC TIMES …
OUR ONLY CHANCE FOR SURVIVAL
LIES IN CREATING OUR OWN LITTLE
ISLANDS OF SANITY AND ORDER,
IN MAKING HAVENS OF OUR HOMES

room, a bathroom incorporating a steam bath, and the beautiful, restful salon.

One of the features of the house is the way roofed-in areas sit alongside areas open to the sky. One moment you are blinded by the desert light outside—the temperature is rarely less than ninety-five degrees Fahrenheit (thirty-five degrees Celsius)—and the next, you are in deep, welcoming shade. And in between are those magical parts of the house where the sunlight filters through lush greenery and antique ironwork grilles to play on the cool, whitewashed walls.

The new extension was not built with any rigid plan in mind, but was designed around

OPPOSITE **In the guests' sitting area, wooden screens and comfortable seating provide a respite from the sun.**
ABOVE LEFT **The mud and straw chimney dominates the open kitchen.**
LEFT **Conical earthenware *tagines*, or cooking pots, have given their name to the dishes cooked in them.**
ABOVE RIGHT **In the scullery, a *couscoussière* is used for couscous, another famous North African dish.**

A HOUSE IS NO HOME UNLESS IT CONTAIN FOOD AND FIRE FOR THE MIND AS WELL AS FOR THE BODY

reclaimed architectural details rummaged from the markets of Morocco—for instance, the iron-work grilles and fanlights. These details succeed in underlining the casual, human, evolving nature of the entire building.

The main salon—open to the garden and to the inner courtyard in order to benefit from any breeze—looks as if it has stood there since time began. Its ceiling, in the old tradition known as *tataoui*, is made of geometrically laid-out eucalyptus and oleander reeds. The whole room, exuding as it does a life subdued by the searing sun and the overwhelming elements, is painted in subtle earth colors. The medina in Marrakesh was combed for the salon's cedar shutters and Turkish kelims, while the leather-covered armchairs, dating from the 1930s when Morocco was a French protectorate and

OPPOSITE In the master bedroom, the four-poster bed has been cleverly created using pillars and a cornice and dome bought from the medina in Marrakesh. The shutters behind the bed open to give enticing views of the garden and to allow cool breezes into the room. In front of the bed stands a marriage trunk that would have been filled with treasures and taken with a bride to her new home.

the property), it pumps this water to a raised reservoir which then overflows into a pool via seven waterfalls. The water from the pool flows into a canal that feeds irrigation channels dug in the soil. These are opened or closed as necessary simply by building up the soil in the channel or by shoveling it out of the way.

Everywhere one goes, whether it be in the house or the garden, one absorbs the feeling of permanence of this old farmhouse, the sense of being close to the earth, the feeling of immense, enveloping quiet. And at night, after the dogs have stopped barking, there is not one single solitary sound to be heard—only silence.

THIS HOUSE IS NOT A VISION OF ARCHITECTURE, BUT … THE TAKING OF AN … OLD FORM AND ADDING … TO CREATE A COZY … RETREAT

ABOVE Thick walls help to keep one of the guest bedrooms in the original farmhouse cool, but thanks to its terracotta paint and the brightly colored locally made textiles, the room has a womblike feel.
RIGHT The bathroom, master bedroom, and salon together form the new L-shaped extension. The bathroom, whose brick cupola has openings for the flow of air, can be filled with steam to make a steam bath, or *hammam*.

reminding one of the country's colonial heritage, were found in a Casablanca flea market. They look serenely somnolent, unlike the formal carved wooden chairs and sofa that are of Syrian design, and the large table found in the souk.

The kitchens of the house are one of its unusual features. The kitchen that lacks a roof—presumably so cooking could be carried on over an open fire without the risk of setting fire to the ceiling—instead boasts a floor made of old tiles, a chimney of mud and straw, and a "cupboard" used for storing wood and with holes that allow the circulation of air. An adjoining scullery features shelves holding a collection of brightly colored Moroccan pottery and a cedarwood door studded with nails that leads into the inner courtyard. The new "closed" kitchen is more up-to-the-minute, with a stove that runs on bottled gas.

An amazing garden has also been created here, much of it thanks to an irrigation system of a type common in North Africa. An electric motor manufactured in Manchester in 1940 is situated in an undergound room. Powered by the constantly flowing fresh water from a well (there is no electricity at

Surrounded by ancient oaks, this solidly built stone cottage has provided protection and escape for its owners since the seventeenth century.

TIMELESS RURAL IDYLL

BELOW **When asked to describe the perfect retreat from the stresses and strains of urban life, a quintessentially English seventeenth-century stone cottage set in woods with streams and ponds effortlessly slips** into mind. This cottage has a tamed wildness about it. It doesn't threaten, but soothes. BELOW LEFT **Up the driveway and across the track lies an idyllic lake with access to more woods and walks.**

This interior designer's escape really is a Great Escape. In the true tradition of romantic literature, she found an ancient English cottage in a sylvan setting in Oxfordshire, with the music of two separate streams running through garden and grounds, and decided that all else was vanity.

Built of local stone some time around 1640, but with eighteenth-century additions, the cottage is actually two workers' homes knocked into one. When the interior designer discovered it, she knew, instinctively, that it was going to be A Project.

For a start, the interior was, for her taste, much too dark—gloomy even. Without sacrificing the character that had attracted her in the first place, she needed to open it up. Though in a pitiful state, it still held the light of other days, and it was this light she seized on.

The first task was to give a greater sense of space on the ground floor by removing the wall between the front and back parlors. This left scope for a large living room with the kitchen at one end, but interestingly, this opening up has not robbed the ground floor of its sense of age and intimacy. The clever grouping of the furniture and

THIS WAS WHAT I PRAYED FOR: A PLOT OF LAND NOT TOO LARGE, CONTAINING A GARDEN, AND NEAR THE HOUSE, A FRESH SPRING OF WATER AND A BIT OF FOREST TO COMPLETE IT

the low beamed ceilings mean that it still feels distinctly cottagey. That, plus the fact that not everything is too perfect. For although the house has been pristinely restored, the uneven walls that have witnessed life over three centuries have sensitively been left untouched.

The color scheme is mainly cream and white, and although much of the furniture is antique, the owner has bravely introduced some new pieces

RIGHT The ground floor of the house was a series of dark interconnecting rooms. By exposing the beams, knocking down a wall, and painting most of the surfaces white, a much brighter atmosphere was created. The wooden floorboards had been hidden under linoleum. In keeping with the simple approach to the interior, they were stripped and lovingly polished.

BELOW By leaving certain walls in place, a cozy living room was created. Furnished with antiques, it provides a change of pace.

LEFT A huge English oak table in the living area is pulled away from the wall when needed for dining, while the wood-burning stove provides easy-to-manage heating.

RIGHT The beautifully aged, mellow, golden Oxfordshire stone has been sensitively restored. The large garden lends itself to spending most of the day outside, either gardening, lunching, or just soaking in the charms of the countryside.

ABOVE **Situated in a glorious rural spot, with rolling hills, ancient woods, and grazing animals, the view from the cottage windows is of the ever-changing backdrop created by the passing seasons. The sounds of the countryside cannot fail to soothe away all city-dweller stress.**
OPPOSITE **As soon as the front door is opened, the cottage's air of calm and timelessness is apparent. The lightness of this area is achieved by a total lack of clutter and the use of simple, organic materials. The focal point of the hall is a stunning modern table whose mellow, natural texture is accentuated at nighttime by soft candlelight.**

whose natural textures and colors blend perfectly with the eighteenth and ninteenth-century oak and mahogany. The overall effect is modern yet comfortable, full of character and lived-in.

Outdoors, the same sure touch is apparent. Enormous effort was put into creating secret little dells, planting flowerbeds, restoring the ancient wall behind the lavender beds, rediscovering the pond, opening up the streams behind their builtup congested banks. All has been freed up and restored in the very best sense of that often abused word.

According to the owner, everything she has done came from the feel of the cottage itself. Now, after much work, she has a retreat that most city-dwellers can only dream of.

ABOVE **The main bedroom continues the cottage's soothing theme with decorations in white and just a hint of color. There is also a continuation of the mix of old and new— a new bedcover but pillows covered in an eighteenth-century toile, picked up in a *brocante* in St. Tropez in the South of France.**
RIGHT **The bathroom with its white-painted tongue-and-groove boards and just a touch of contrasting color in the gray towels and floorboards, is a hymn to simplicity—a room in which to restore oneself completely.**

WATERSIDE ESCAPES

The sound of lapping water at the edge of a lake or on the seashore is one of the most harmonious sounds known to the human ear. It seems to answer a deep-seated call of the soul, reminding us that although we are mortal, there are some things in this mysterious world of ours that are neverending.

But although our lakes and oceans go on forever, they are not unchanging. Shifts in the weather can have a sudden, dramatic effect. One minute the sky gleams azure, there is a light breeze, and gentle clear blue waves run unruffled up against the shore. The next, the heavens are blocked out by thick gray cloud, a wind is whipped up, and the waves lash their fury at our feet.

This library of amazing sounds and sights is extended by a selection of unmistakable smells—the tang of crisp, salty ocean air; the clean, balmy odor of trees and flowers carried in on soft breezes over still lakes. Water calls to us, and we respond by nesting on its shores, but to build a home there requires the same sensitivity to and respect for that most changeable of elements that every sailor must learn.

The waterside homes featured here have all been built with a consciousness of the beauty and unpredictability of water in mind. They are very different, but each is a haven of tranquility. Many of their owners have been driven to the waterside by their desire to recapture childhood memories of idyllic summers spent swimming, boating, sunbathing, and picknicking there—a stress-free time when the living was easy.

The first of these homes belongs to a couple who write and illustrate children's books. Their weatherboarded house at the water's edge in England's East Anglia almost looks like a boat riding the waves, untouched by time just like the place it inhabits. By contrast, in Malibu on America's West Coast, a talented English designer has created a cool, minimal home that looks out meditatively over the vast expanse of the Pacific Ocean. In Mexico, again alongside the Pacific, a renowned architect has built himself a unique native-style family retreat that welcomes in the ocean on one side and the jungle on the other, while the calm shores of Lake Placid play host to a lovingly rebuilt and lovingly used wooden Great Camp. Nothing could be more different from this than the boldly modern house sitting atop a windy English cliff facing the Atlantic Ocean, or the old white-painted fisherman's house overlooking the ancient Moroccan port of Asilah. There is no doubt—waterside living provides something to suit every mood.

The Boathouse looks like a boathouse, but this is just a happy illusion. What is more, it gives the impression that it is about to set sail on the morning tide of the East Anglian estuary where it has stood since just after the World War I, but this, too, is an illusion.

In fact, when the present owners first came across it, the Boathouse was a solidly embedded part of the picturesque East Anglian waterscape. There it stood, serene in the midst of a motley collection of huts and houseboats, the center of a sort of seaside shanty town.

It immediately struck a chord with this writer-and-illustrator team of countless children's books, one of whom had been brought up on this very coast. What was more, the Boathouse was for sale. Here, on this comparatively remote coast, far from the hurlyburly of city life, the couple decided to stage their retreat. This was a place where they could write, paint, watch the tides, and sleep to the sound of water on three sides.

On this eastern seaboard, beloved by the British Royal Family who, traditionally, have come here in search of healthy sea breezes, the amusements have remained gentle and decorous. In fact, you can be forgiven for thinking that nothing has happened here since about 1948.

Certainly, nothing much has happened to the Boathouse. In a previous existence, it was owned by an elderly lady with a butler and a very individualistic approach to life. The butler's quarters were in the porch, suitably curtained off.

The memory of this eccentric habitation lives on under its new custodians. With the sensitiivity of the artist they have, wisely, left much alone. For example, they have retained a doughty square-armed sofa and chairs, together with the sentimental Edwardian prints—"Granny's Christmas Visitors" is one example—and vases of grasses dried in Coronation year—1953—in the bedroom. They've also kept the verses by Rudyard Kipling alongside words by Patience Strong on the bathroom walls, admonishing the denizens of the Boathouse to "Gather every shining hour."

But they have made changes, for instance by adding an upper floor. This is a single lookout room with windows all around. Its atmosphere is reminiscent of that of the sun lounge on board a

The Boathouse feels as if it belongs on this particular stretch of East Anglian coast. There is something quintessentially refined, unchanging, and English about the scene. While, over recent years, more intrepid travelers have headed for sun and sea in foreign climes, many have been content to escape to the peace and tranquility of this quiet English spot, with only the lapping of the sea and the calls of the gulls for company.

BOATHOUSE BELLE

Surrounded by the ever-changing sea and intimately affected by its moods, the Boathouse stands like a bastion between shore and sea.

LEFT **The bustling setting of the Boathouse has long been that of a busy English sailing and fishing center. Surrounded by water on three sides, the house is jostled by boats of all sizes and colors, and in varying states of repair—sailing dinghies, old-fashioned rowing boats, and working fishing boats.**

NOW THE GREAT WINDS SHOREWARD BLOW,

NOW THE SALT TIDES SEAWARDS FLOW;

NOW THE WILD WHITE HORSES PLAY,

CHAMP AND CHAFE AND TOSS IN THE SPRAY

ABOVE **In the downstairs living room with its white-painted walls, much of the furniture was inherited from previous owners. The Delft tiles on the wall behind the Coalbrookdale stove were found on a construction site.**

grand pre-World War I ocean liner. Sitting here on the elegant wicker furniture, the view is of endless water, up the estuary or out to the North Sea. And, because in this part of the world the north wind blows straight in from Scandinavia, there's a huge Scandinavian-style stove decorated with Delft tiles to warm yourself by.

This inspiring room is reached by a spiral wooden staircase redolent of alpine chalets but actually acquired at a sale in Sussex and, with their unerring eye for discarded treasures, the owners similarly swooped on an old train refrigerator, now happily installed in a crucial corner.

Under the protective East Anglian sky, the Boathouse today is still a place where Kipling or Patience Strong would have been at home.

THERE IS NOTHING … HALF SO
MUCH WORTH DOING AS SIMPLY
MESSING ABOUT IN BOATS

The Boathouse and its environs exude a powerful sense of 1940s and 1950s coastal England. Britons now in their forties and fifties who as children were taken to places like this for their annual seaside vacation can relate to such an atmosphere. Here they can sink back into that gentle nostalgia, where the sun shone all day and the sea was always warm. The present owners of the house have done all they can to retain that ambience, turning their home into a refuge where comfort and tradition lend a feeling of permanence and belonging. The Boathouse is also somewhere to enjoy the all-pervading presence of the sea—from the sound of lapping waves, to the cries of sea birds, to the smell of fish and seaweed. These are the elements that never change—the continuum of life.

LEFT Suspended between two grand Malibu beach properties stands the small but perfectly formed White Barn.
BELOW In the main living area, the legs of a console table are made of wood from an eighteenth-century barn while the top was commissioned in Indonesia.
RIGHT An antique Indonesian wooden bowl made on the island of Lambok and inlaid with mother-of-pearl commands attention as it leans nonchalantly against a white-painted wall.
OPPOSITE Standing in front of the open fireplace, a nineteenth-century Indian bed makes an original coffee table. The fireplace holds a woven basket from Indonesia, the pots above are wood and come from the Philippines, while the reclaimed cabinet doors alongside are dry-brushed for a distressed look.

MINIMAL IN MALIBU

Not far from the jungle that is Los Angeles, the White Barn gazes out over the mighty Pacific Ocean, providing a serene minimalist haven from the commercialization and stresses of modern life.

The great motto in life of the English woman who owns "the white barn on the beach" is the minimalist one—less is more. No wonder then that her house is the exemplification of minimalism.

Malibu—where her interior-design company office is located — was the natural choice for her home. With its magnificent coastline, its tranquility that rides in on the waves from the Pacific, it is within striking distance of Los Angeles, but happily distant from its din and bustle.

The house, when she found it, was nothing more than a tiny cottage, and plainly this would not do. So she "put the house in a dumpster" and started again from scratch. After filling a dumpster or twelve, she could start to fashion her dream.

That dream started many years before when she lived in Barbados. Here she discovered that life is largely governed by climate and that the effect of sunlight on wood, of salt in the air, dictate the decor both indoors and out. In Barbados she learned, too, about uncluttered living, about surrounding yourself only with what you love, and about discarding the unnecessary.

Now fast-forward some years to Malibu. Staying in a beach house with her film-producer husband, she was out walking one day along the beach. And there it was. A rundown little cottage, with low ceilings and tiny boxy rooms.

LEFT **By creating a tranquil atmosphere with the use of white-painted tongue-and-groove boards and exposed, white-painted beams and rafters, the designer has made sure that the eye is drawn to focal points like these two oak plinths. They come from an eighteenth-century Vermont barn and are surmounted by a pair of massive California-made beeswax candles, and by two framed photographs by Joan Armand.**

BELOW LEFT **Walking from the bedrooms toward the living room, one is rewarded with a grand view of the huge floor-to-ceiling window.**

OPPOSITE **The kitchen continues the peaceful, neutral theme, with white cabinets and pale maplewood counters. Once again, there is an array of woven baskets and beautiful wooden bowls from Indonesia. A pure white orchid adds another oriental touch. Light pours in from the bedrooms and through the wall opening high under the rafters.**

The realtor who showed her around summed her up at a glance. He cleverly took her in via the garage. This was a relator with instinct, for there, in the garage, was a high pitched roof with exposed beams and rafters. Immediately she could see light and the potential for peace. Within hours, the contract was signed and sealed. "The white barn on the beach" was already starting to grow in her imagination.

Now, after gutting and rebuilding, the small, poky-roomed house has been transformed into one enormous peaceful space, approximately 40 × 50 feet (12 × 15 meters) and dominated by a huge floor-to-ceiling window. It incorporates living and dining areas and a kitchen and, leading off the kitchen, a master bedroom and guest bedroom, each with its own bathroom. While the bedrooms and bathrooms have normal-height ceilings and an intimate feel, the main space is high-ceilinged with white-painted boards and rafters that tilt at a multitude of different angles, allowing the wonderful West Coast light that floods in from the sea to bounce back and forth as the day progresses. High up among the rafters and set against that amazing window is the most peaceful area—the Zen den—reached by a hidden ladder and offering spectacular views of the Pacific Ocean.

From the outside the house is equally inspiring. Viewed from the road, crammed in between its larger neighbors, it looks like nothing. But seen from the sea, you enter a completely different world. This is a climate where life is lived

IF YOU WANT A GOLDEN RULE THAT WILL FIT EVERYBODY, THIS IS IT: HAVE NOTHING IN YOUR HOUSES THAT YOU DO NOT KNOW TO BE USEFUL, OR BELIEVE TO BE BEAUTIFUL

ABOVE **The overall whiteness of the decor and the clever juxtaposition of old and new, and materials from all over the world, blend seamlessly together. In this corner, a nineteenth-century Chinese armoire, a painting of the owner, and a planed and waxed table from Vermont oak create a cozy winter or bad-weather dining space.**
RIGHT **A mirror framed by plants casts a reflection of the depth of the house, and of the sea beyond.**

excess. It is an oasis of monastic calm, a journey into peace. The white ceilings and walls add to this sense, but they also serve to focus attention on the few carefully chosen, exquisite objects from Indonesia, from China, from anywhere in the Far East. There are Indonesian woven baskets in natural colors and many sizes, wooden bowls from the Philippines, a beautifully carved antique Indian wooden bed that does duty as a coffee table. These pieces speak of craftsmanship, of people's history, of hardship. In this cocoon of pure whiteness and light, nothing is there for nothing.

The second thing to strike you when you enter is the neatness. Where are the books, the CDs, the magazines, the clothes, the clutter of everyday life? Needless to say, these have all been reduced to a minimum; then that minimum has been cleverly stowed away so as not to detract from the ordered calm that pervades every

IN ALL CIRCUMSTANCES, HOWEVER HARD THEY MAY BE, WE SHOULD REJOICE RATHER THAN BE CAST DOWN, THAT WE MAY NOT LOSE THE GREATEST GOOD, THE PEACE AND TRANQUILITY OF OUR SOUL

as much outdoors as in, so the exterior space has been designed rather like a series of outdoor rooms.

Steps lead up from the beach to a wooden deck used for entertaining. From here the view of the house is at its most beguiling, with its two pitched roofs and huge arched window giving the house something of a fairytale appearance. More steps take you down to the broad expanse of stone and brick terrace, where a welcoming dining table stands beneath a lushly overgrown arbor. Here, with the sound of the pounding waves in the background, friends regularly gather for relaxed *al fresco* meals. Cross the terrace, go up a few more steps, and you reach the back door that leads into the main living area. It has been an exhilarating stroll.

As soon as you enter the house, one thing that strikes you is the sheer whiteness and the lack of

ABOVE AND LEFT **Above the main living space and reached by a hidden ladder is a sleeping platform or "Zen den." From this white cocoon, the owners can enjoy views of the Pacific breakers. The sense of escape is complete.**

RIGHT **In the master bedroom, an early American naive painting of a sheep holds court over a perfectly plain stained ebony bed with white sheets. The table, with a single, meditational bloom, is from the Philippines.**

**In California, no escape is
complete without a
terrace, wooden deck, and
views of the sea, but one
has to be conscious of the
effects of harsh sunlight. At
the White Barn, cane
tables and chairs stand on
the beachside wooden
deck, while on the stone
and brick terrace, a large
flower-bedecked arbor
makes the perfect outdoor
dining room. A blind can be
rolled down for protection
from the sun. A collection
of plant-filled terracotta
pots flourish alongside.
BELOW Viewed from the
terrace, the White Barn
flaunts a huge floor-to-
ceiling arched window,
with just a hint of the East
Coast in its roof covered in
wooden shingles.**

corner. You would be hard-pressed to notice that a Chinese armoire cun-
ningly conceals a music system and collection of CDs. Or that the dry-
brushed doors alongside the fireplace hide books and magazines. A number
of massive Indonesian wooden boxes in the bedrooms and in a corner of the
living room play host to the store of spare bedlinen; the corridor linking the
kitchen and the bedrooms is lined with closets for household paraphernalia;
while a walk-in clothes closet has been neatly fitted in next to the main
bathroom. A private detective could not have concealed himself better.

During the mild Pacific-lapped winters, this all-white heaven is warmed by
just a few touches of carefully chosen color. Indian handwoven and paisley
throws and pillow covers in tones of rich red and dark earth grace the sofas
and chairs; dark red candles stand on trays of coffee beans; and glass vases
shimmer full of red kidney beans.

And now the house acts as a magnet for friends
and acquaintances. Visitors look around, sigh wistfully,
and say, "Can I have one like this please? Can I have
a life where I'm not bothered by *things*?" And so the
owner of the White Barn began to "do" the homes
of her friends, in her own particular, gentle, unobtru-
sive way. And from all of this has grown her highly
successful interior-design company—from an expatriate youth spent in Barbados and an old garage.

MEXICAN COASTAL JUNGLE RETREAT

Poised between jungle and ocean, this traditionally constructed complex exists in perfect harmony with nature.

Every three weeks or so, the Mexican in our story leaves behind him the dust, noise, and vigor of Mexico City and, with his wife and grown-up family, decamps to the sea. It is a journey that involves a flight, a drive by four-wheel truck, the fording of a river that may or may not be impassable depending on the vagaries of the weather, then a final, triumphant haul along a dirt

track with the jungle slowly closing in around them. And then, there it is—the beach house on the Pacific Coast—surely like no other. The family's Great Escape. This Great Escape must be one of the grandest and most exotic beach houses ever conceived by lover of sea, sky, and locations so remote as to be almost eerie.

The beach house is, in fact, a succession of huts built by its architect-owner on the principle of native Mexican villages, with their beautiful high roofs, or *palapas*, made from palms. From the violet ocean the house looks

Drawing on native Mexican architecture, this idyllic escape on the rocky shore of the Pacific looks from the ocean like a traditional village. But under the influence of the Mexican architect Luis Barragán, it has a distinctly modern feel. Its seventeen pink 23-foot (seven-meter) high, 10-foot (three-meter) wide columns, set 6½ feet (2 meters) apart, rather than acting as a barrier to the jungle, seem to want it to encroach. This is a magical place where ocean and jungle have been tamed only temporarily.

THE VOICE OF THE SEA SPEAKS TO THE SOUL. THE TOUCH OF THE SEA IS SENSUOUS, ENFOLDING THE BODY IN ITS SOFT, CLOSE EMBRACE

like a row of pyramids rising from the dense jungle vegetation. And the site was chosen with this in mind, so there would be nothing but rampant vegetation on one side, and the huge, ever-changing ocean on the other.

The whole complex was designed to capture these stunning views, and with openings in the side walls at all angles beneath the shade of the *palapas*, not one is lost. The main living area is found beneath the largest *palapa*—a beach hut on a truly grand scale. Next in size, and separated from the living area by broad steps, is the dining-room *palapa*. Together with the kitchen *palapa*, these are the only communal spaces.

Ten smaller *palapa*-topped structures contain the bedrooms and their bathrooms. These are

The main living area, with its floors and sofa bases made from concrete set with marble chips, is where the family congregates. It nestles under the largest *palapa*. As in Mexican Indian villages, this is the complex's main focus. Along with the large dining area and the kitchen beneath other *palapas*, it provides the only communal space. Open to the elements, the living room enjoys spectacular views on all sides. With locally made chairs and stools, and with its giant sculpted stone shells, the area is ideal for relaxation.

dotted about over the sloping site, their pointed roofs piercing the horizon at a variety of levels. Some of them are double-story, with winding interior stairways leading to the bathrooms above. All have magnificent views out over both jungle and ocean.

The structure of the complex is almost monastic, but far from bleak. On the contrary, the architect-owner has been careful to introduce a wealth of color—the strawberry-pink columns that greet you as you arrive from the jungle, the candy-pink colorwash in one of the bedrooms, the orange-painted steps between the living and dining areas.

And then there are the plants and shells for ornamentation, providing a link with the outdoors. Huge palms and cacti can scarcely be contained in their earthenware pots. Enormous shell sculptures, specially commissioned from a local artist, mimic the shells lying scattered on the seashore.

Although many of the complex's structures are made of concrete, the architect pays homage to local building traditions by topping them with tall, conical thatched roofs, or *palapas*. These are made from palm fronds, cut and treated during the full moon when the sap is at its most abundant. There is something calming and mystical about them and, as well as being beautiful, they also serve a practical purpose for they allow the heat to rise, while beneath, the open sides of the huts gather in the cooling sea breezes. The architect has also been at pains to make sure the visitor is aware of the power of the natural environment. The artificial swimming pool is deliberately diminutive: the great bottomless blue ocean stretching to the distant horizon is the real pool. Swimming in the smaller one, we can only wonder at the vast immensity of nature.

Crammed with these delights and with their open sides capturing every passing breeze, the interiors are an organic part of the remarkable outside world.

There in the jungle, luscious vegetation crowded with birds presses in from all directions. There are hummingbirds, butterflies of every size and color, scorpions, and enormous armies of ants. The ground seems to be alive with their constant movement. Or look out over that wonderful ocean, where the eye is constantly delighted by the sea-life—the pelicans, those most caring of creatures, teaching their young to fish, drying their wings on the rocks, the crabs laboriously crawling over the sand, the seagulls whirling in the unbelievably blue skies above.

Lying awake at night, immersed in a good book, the delighted guest is visited by a jungle bird who has flown in under the roof. Or before going to bed, there's the opportunity to take a starlit swim from the sanctuary of a

THERE IS A PLEASURE IN THE PATHLESS WOODS,
THERE IS A RAPTURE ON THE LONELY SHORE,
THERE IS SOCIETY, WHERE NONE INTRUDES, BY THE DEEP SEA, AND MUSIC IN ITS ROAR:
I LOVE NOT MAN THE LESS, BUT NATURE MORE

garden bedroom. And all this to the lulling of the waves on the rocky shore, the feeling of absolute apartness from the busy, breakneck world beyond.

Everywhere in this extraordinary complex, the genius of its visionary architect-owner in marrying the modern with the vernacular, shines through. Here are contemporary buildings that are completely at home with their surroundings. But while savoring the ocean breezes, the jungle scents, while witnessing the ever-present wildlife, one is ever aware of the uniqueness of the situation—of being sandwiched precariously between jungle and ocean. This is a house which, at any moment, could be snatched back, either by the luxuriant, encroaching jungle, or by the whim of the waves.

Ten smaller *palapas* shelter the bedrooms with their bathrooms, all at different levels above the ocean and all with terraces. Here guests can sit undisturbed and marvel at the natural surroundings. The massive louvered doors can be opened to give views of the jungle, the gardens, the ocean, or the small inlets cutting into the coastline.

The monastic white simplicity of the bedrooms is broken by splashes of color on the bedlinen, the lines of cobblestones set into the floors, and in the crushed strawberry pigment used in the passages. Furnishings are kept to a minimum—this is, after all, an escape from the clutter of city life—so the eye is drawn instead to the drama of the great outdoors on every side. The importance of privacy and seclusion to the owner is very evident in the siting of these bedroom suites. Although enjoying wonderful vistas, they are not overlooked. Sitting on their terraces, one feels totally alone, with only the sounds of the wildlife and the waves, and glimpses of small local fishing boats to remind one of the presence of other beings.

To find this house—or camp as it is called in the Adirondacks—on Lake Placid in the north of New York state, you have to first find a village on Lake Placid, then a peninsula, then finally cross a strait to an island. In a world where travel has become very simple, there is a pioneering spirit to be found in the Adirondacks, if only because the camps close down in September and don't open again until the following Easter. The development of the camps started around 1872: Lake Placid was one of the first areas in the Adirondacks to witness them. During the next thirty years, over a hundred camps sprang up on the lake shore and its islands. The lake was known as "Peerless Placid" and "The Gem of the Adirondacks." This camp is perched precariously on the slopes of an island, with wonderful views from its terraces and boathouse over the lake, virgin forests, and mountain ranges.

PLACID LAKESIDE RENDEZVOUS

Strong, solid, and remote— there is something of the pioneer about this island house on an Adirondack lake.

The wooden house—traditionally known in the Adirondacks as a camp—situated on Lake Placid was just crying out for love, affection, and a big happy family to bring its gloomy, dilapidated rooms back to life. It found all this and more in the husband and wife who bought the old camp on the island on a wing and a prayer. It was crumbling, unmortgagable, and totally and utterly piteous. But they—expatriates, uprooted and living in Frankfurt—had such a strong urge to get away from city life and back to a simpler way of being, that this rundown place tottering on its crumbling foundations on Buck Island immediately seemed the answer.

In her childhood, the wife had spent a part of each summer on a small lake and some time in the Adirondacks. She cherished memories of swimming, boating, hiking, and just living the outdoor life. He, Danish, and with a great love of boats and boating, similarly yearned for a life without any hint of glitz, one that would hark back to sunlit summers and the open air. And, as expatriates, they both needed and wanted a place where they could have their families and friends around them for as long as possible.

They knew they could find all this at Lake Placid, but it would have to be just a house for the summer, for in winter the lake freezes over. In late fall, the last of the blazing autumn foliage falling from the trees would mark the end of their idyllic retreat until next summer.

But to enjoy any idyllic summers there, like the wealthy New York families—the Rockefellers, for example—who had first discovered and developed the Adirondacks, they had some major structural problems to address. Problems

like the foundations. The house had to be lifted, have new foundations established, and then set down square again. During this painful process, they discovered rotten walls that simply had to be torn down. But out of evil cometh good. Now, instead of numerous small rooms, they could enjoy open, unobstructed spaces, totally at one with the feel of the lake.

Finally, they have just what they wanted: a warm welcoming home that can sleep a multitude and which, they hope, will stand the test of time, providing many happy summers for their children and their children's children.

OPPOSITE In this massively forested region, the natural building material was wood, and the early builders developed a unique regional style. Wooden decks, walkways, and terraces provide unsurpassed views of the natural surroundings.
ABOVE When the owners are in the Adirondacks for their family break, one of the aims of their escape is to spend as much time as possible in "the great outdoors." Simple furniture adorns the deck of the house so meals can be taken *al fresco*.
ABOVE RIGHT With its narrower boards and smaller window, the top bedroom is part of the original old camp.
RIGHT By contrast, the master bedroom is light and airy with doors leading onto the terrace. The interior is simple and uncluttered, enjoying glimpses of the mountains and lakes on all sides.

ATLANTIC BASTION

Gently fortified against the Atlantic storms, Baggy House gazes defiantly out to sea. Technology, a keen sense of design, and a respect for the natural environment make this a unique family home.

Baggy House sits facing the sea, defiantly astride the North Devon cliffs. Set amid a garden tumbling down the cliff face, the Atlantic Ocean side of Baggy House, with its floating, light, transparent appearance, has been designed so it conducts a dialogue with the craggy, vernacular style of construction of the other side. The side facing the ocean boasts finely finished woods and metals in contrast to the rougher finishes used on the far side of the house.

The owners of Baggy House are forever conscious of the fact that, when the wind, rain, and storms come tearing in from the Atlantic Ocean, this bold house is the first thing in their path. When they created it, they knew that it had to be built as if for a battle. And battle it indeed is, as the tempests rage, but the house stands firm.

From their many visits to this part of Devon, in Southwestern England, a place they already loved, the pair of London professionals were all too aware of the gale-force winds common to the area and the problems they posed. They realized they would have to contend with them, but they are people who do not shrink from the insurmountable. They knew what they wanted: to live with the elements; to look out on the Atlantic and have nothing between it and them but glass. Anthony Hudson of Hudson Featherstone

The central core of the house is the main living area, dominated by spectacular views of the ocean and Lundy Island. Airy balustrades made of rope and zinc-sprayed steel give a feeling of being on an ocean liner, while the curved copper ceiling over the dining area extends beyond the window to become a verdigrised canopy sheltering an outdoor sitting area. Much of the furniture was specially commissioned.

Architects was chosen to realize a dream that would combine the ancient and the modern, and with his vision and expertise, plus the owners' bold, headlong approach, the old 1930s hotel that stood on the site was pulled down and the award-winning Baggy House was born.

From the sea Baggy House looks as if it is floating. The materials chosen for this side are light and translucent—glass and finely finished metal and woodwork. If the owners had had their way, they would have had nothing but glass here, but technically this was an impossibility, so compromises had to be made. The result is a huge window—it weighs a ton—in the living room, that slides into the ground by means of a button, an electric motor, and a system constructed by a local company specializing in food-lifting equipment. With the window down, the brave house stands open to the elements. The effect is wondrous, but with three small children, the owners had to prevent the window from being opened and the children rushing headlong to the sea. The solution was ingenious—the button works only when a key is simultaneously inserted in an out-of-the-way slot.

At the rear of the house, Hudson was at pains to give a sense of its being rooted in the ground, of hugging the earth. Here, he used a construction

THEY THAT GO DOWN TO THE SEA IN SHIPS, AND OCCUPY THEIR BUSINESS IN GREAT WATERS, THESE SEE THE WORKS OF THE LORD AND HIS WONDERS IN THE DEEP

FAR LEFT The entrance hall is dominated by a granite megalith reflected in a floor-to-ceiling mirror.
FAR LEFT, CENTER A porthole window in a door provides a glimpse of the American oak kitchen.
FAR LEFT, BELOW The exterior door is made of planks backed with lead.
LEFT Old and new, heavy and light meet in the kitchen. A stone butler's sink is complemented by a stainless steel one set in a glass counter, and a traditional wooden plate rack hangs opposite suspended steel shelving.

method that was more traditional, and finishes that are rougher, craggier, more earthy. Unlike the other side, where a white finish is used, the back is painted terracotta. The front door leads into a dark, lowering hall where a granite megalith supports the massive chimney stack and the rear of the house. With its slate floor, this is a primeval place, almost subterranean in feel, but as you walk toward the main living and dining area, there is an explosion of light culminating in the most magnificent ocean view.

Other, smaller details of the interior are no less inspiring. Openings of various shapes are set into the walls to provide fleeting glimpses of the ever-changing sea and sky. There are natural materials and textures everywhere, from massive oak panels above the fireplace, limestone flooring in the dining room, an enormous polished solid maplewood column in the sitting area that

ABOVE In contrast to the open living area, the master bedroom with its oak headboard has a womblike, intimate feel.
RIGHT The blue-tiled main bathroom shows the influence of Islamic architecture. Here, a limestone floor introduces an organic element to the glass, tiles, and steel. The room feels totally private, although the circular skylight brings the outdoors in, showing times of day and changing weather patterns.

supports the upper floors, and, to contrast, delicate curtain panels of hand-painted silk that slide away into wooden cupboards on each side of that famous window. Then there are the lead-clad ceilings and the cast-glass stair treads that lead upstairs, where friends with families can stay in suites of rooms with interconnecting doors.

In the garden, the most striking feature is the swimming pool, designed by Anthony Hudson and his partner, Sarah Featherstone. With its barbecue, dining area, and dressing rooms, its splashing waterfall and its underwater tunnels leading from the main pool to the children's pool—demarcated by a wooden deck and slate causeway—this is a place for pure fun and enjoyment.

Although it is only a few years old, Baggy House has become a cynosure for visitors to the north Devon coast and spectators are encouraged. For the couple who own it, this is not just their Great Escape, but a monument to modern architecture, one that they hope will stand for generations to come. And the green-blue Atlantic will still be crashing at the door.

With its vivid color and sculptural concrete, the startling thing about the swimming pool is that it adorns the coastline of **North Devon** and not that of Mexico or Miami. The pool, on the site of a sunken rose garden, is sheltered by boulders and tamarisk trees, which grow well on the coasts of **South Africa**, **California**, and, apparently, **North Devon!** The tumbling waterfall echoes the pounding sea below, while the combination of limestone, slate, and cedar bring warmth, helped by the constantly maintained eighty degrees of the water. The views from the house across pool and ocean are simply breathtaking.

OPPOSITE **From the top terrace, reached by steep white stairs, the great Atlantic fills the view as far as the eye can see. A guest bedroom and this cool sitting area occupy the top story. Here, where sea meets sky, flapping canvas sails shade the painted cement terrace from the overhead sun. The decoration of the terrace, with its fabrics, traditional pierced-metal lanterns bought in Tangier, and the wire glass holder, demonstrate the owners' interest in local crafts.**
LEFT **From one corner of the terrace there is a view of a picturesque, domed marabout, or Muslim holy man's shrine, and a Maronite cemetery.**

A fisherman's house in Asilah looks lazily out over the Atlantic. The sounds of the sea mix with street shouts and calls to prayer from the mosque.

BLUE OCEAN-LAPPED PARADISE

The French chatelaine of this beautiful, restful retreat and her husband had traveled for years through Morocco, but it was only when they saw the fisherman's house standing right in the medina but facing the majestic Atlantic in the old Portuguese port of Asilah that they thought, "We've found it. This is where we want to be."

Just 28 miles (45 kilometers) from Tangier, this fabled medieval town was constructed on the foundations of the old Phoenician city of Stilis.

With its fourteenth-century walls built by the Portuguese as protection from the encroachments of the sea, the place immediately appealed to her and her architect husband.

When they first bought the house, it was just a ground floor with a partly destroyed courtyard. The two of them gazed at the fig tree in the courtyard and made a tough decision. The tree would have to go. But then they changed their minds. After all, who had got there first? Finally

BELOW **The fisherman's cottage stands alongside the ramparts of the medina on the Atlantic Ocean side. Despite having been built six hundred years ago, these sturdy walls still stand firm. The blue of sea and sky, and the white of the buildings, are the town's natural colors. In the narrow, winding streets of the medina, pockets of shade provide relief from the intensity of the sun, while the small windows, thick walls, and shutters of the upstairs windows of the houses provide some comfort for their occupants. Downstairs windows are protected by metal grilles.**

LEFT **One of the bedrooms on the new second floor has a lovely airy feel. The cement floor is bare, so attention is concentrated on the few rich decorative details, most of which have been bought locally. The two couchs, which double as beds, are covered with beautiful rugs. Above one of them, three small ironwork animals bought in the flea market stand in simple niches, while the window opposite is dressed with curtains made of blue and white** *fouta* **fabric. A dainty wall lamp made of white-painted pierced concrete is typical of the work of Asilah.**

OPPOSITE AND BELOW LEFT **Between the two bedrooms on the first floor there is a central balcony looking out to the sea, where breakfast is eaten beneath the canvas awning. The white wickerwork chairs contribute to the sense of being on board a yacht, with the wind straining at the canvas and the sounds and smells of the ocean.**

BELOW RIGHT **The view of the sea from the terrace.**

Walking through the medina and past the Pirates' Palace that hugs the ancient sea walls, the entrance to the house is through a nondescript door in the white walls. Inside, a small hallway leads through to an interior courtyard open to the sky. This is the heart of the original fisherman's cottage, although it has been much enlarged. It is dominated by an old fig tree that previously stood against what was the end wall of the house. Now the tree is central to the courtyard—or summer dining area—and provides shade from the intense midday sun. Despite the fierce climate, a mass of white-painted pots brimful of plants creates a sense of lushness. The white walls and painted terracotta floor are typical of local design. This courtyard is the one area of the house that is totally private. The sounds of the street and the sea are strangely muted, and the position of the sun dictates where you can sit, eat, read, and rest.

they decided that they would just have to mold the house around the tree. So, with a wry respect for the past, they proceeded to draw up plans for what would be their great escape.

Incorporating two extra storys to give magnificent views of the rolling Atlantic was their first priority. The ground floor, which was nothing more than two rooms, would also be enlarged. This would provide them with a winter dining room and living room in the original buildings, and, with the courtyard extended, they could also have an outdoor summer dining room.

They drew up their plans and presented them to the Moroccan workforce, who set to work with enthusiasm. Now, with the addition of the two

FAR RIGHT In a corner of the courtyard, a table surrounded by built-in seating is laid for traditional Arabic mint tea. The Moroccan silver, metalware, and glassware were found in the souk, where many local fishermen sell paintings they have made. The owners are constantly looking for new purchases.

LEFT AND RIGHT
By extending the old courtyard to encompass a room from the cottage next door, the owners now have a large outdoor dining area, perfect for summer evenings. The extension of the courtyard also provided the space for steps to the balconies above, while still retaining the traditional courtyard feel. In one corner of the courtyard, a cement shelf is home to a collection of lanterns and a pair of pictures by a local artist.

I WAS SET FREE! I DISSOLVED IN THE SEA, BECAME WHITE SAILS AND FLYING SPRAY, BECAME BEAUTY AND RHYTHM, BECAME MOONLIGHT AND THE SHIP AND THE HIGH DIM-STARRED SKY. I BELONGED, WITHOUT PAST OR FUTURE WITHIN PEACE AND UNITY AND A WILD JOY

extra floors and a set of terraces, stairs, and gangways that look as if they have just come from an ocean liner, the house is finished. Blue paintwork and the lavish use of the blue and white fabric used in the *fouta*, or overskirts worn by the women in the mountains, echo the vivid blue of Asilah's sea and sky.

And, while the Parisian owners have taken great pains to equip the house with locally made furnishings, textiles, and artefacts, there are, not surprisingly, a few European influences to be detected. Among these are ceramics brought from France but in colors inspired by Morocco, paintings by Europeans, but again inspired by Morocco, and a beautiful bench in the living room, made locally from a design by the English designer Teddy Millington-Drake.

Sitting on the terrace there's a view of a distant mosque, the hum of voices comes rising up from the street below, and, above all, there is the sound and smell of the sea. This is a house that's forever open to the life outside, where there's always sight of the ocean and where the

LEFT AND RIGHT **Located in the original part of the house, this winter living room is typical of Morocco—long and narrow with a high ceiling and a tiny window, so it is cool in summer and easy to heat during cold winter nights.**

The carved wooden bench was made locally to a design by Teddy Millington-Drake, but the fabrics covering it are antique. Bought in the souk, the old mirror above the bench reflects a view of the courtyard outside.

from the street outside through a simple, almost hidden door. Upstairs it is possible to revel in the open aspect from terrace and balcony, while downstairs are the house's secluded, private areas. There is nothing direct, brusque, or untoward anywhere. On the contrary, the mood of the place is oblique, subtle, unhurried.

And now these inspired creators have a dream house that offers them both an active and a contemplative life. In short, it is a brilliant recreation of the paradoxically open yet secretive Moroccan way of life that they had long admired from their very different Parisian home.

owners are regularly reminded of why they came from Paris to this magical place.

And, because the house stands in the medina, there's a constant invitation to mingle with the vibrant life of the surrounding streets. In the old square, children play football or untwist long skeins of thread for their mothers' embroidery, while in the alleyways people meet to gossip, sometimes shaded from the burning sun by rose or vine-covered trellises. The *trompe l'oeil* effect of doors and windows painted on blank white walls makes it a place of total visual delight.

But while much of the life of the medina goes on in the street, there is also a sense of another private, enclosed life there, the life of the Muslim families that takes place behind the walls and closed doors. And the fisherman's house that was reflects that inner landscape, too. Its courtyard, built around the famous fig tree, is the summer dining area, open to the elements; but to enter the house, one has to approach

BLUE COLOR IS EVERLASTINGLY APPOINTED BY THE DEITY TO BE A SOURCE OF DELIGHT

ABOVE **On the second floor, the small shower room is contructed from local materials. The fretted doors are made locally, and the tiles, known as *zeliges*, are from Fez.**
LEFT **This tiny room is the original winter dining room. The fabrics are local; the carpet was bought on a trip to the Atlas Mountains; and the stools come from the market. Whitewash mixed with pigments from the souk covers the walls.**

MOUNTAIN & HILLSIDE ESCAPES

The nearest place to heaven is surely on top of a mountain, within a fingertip's reach of the sky. Perhaps that is why many spiritual retreats—in Tibet and Nepal, for instance—are located in mountainous regions, for here the clarity of the air, the purity of the silence, and the daunting beauty of the landscape conspire to make an environment that is almost otherworldly.

Practically speaking, mountain and hilltops have also always been strategic locations for the building of castles and fortresses, and places for people to seek refuge from the enemy. Throughout history warlords, kings, and queens have taken advantage of these sites. From them, their guards could see at a glance from whence the foe rode.

But fortunately, in modern times and in most parts of the world, other humans are no longer the enemy. Today, it is the stress of modern life we try to escape from, the horrible feeling that, for so many of us, work has become home, and home, work. That is why each owner of these mountain or hillside escapes has mentally pulled up the drawbridge.

In the heart of Mexico, in a spot known for centuries as a place of spiritual healing, a perceptive sculptor has added his own personal statement to the volcanic landscape.

It takes the form of a star-shaped concrete home whose stairway to heaven surely helps its owner on his spiritual journey. In Sicily, two ancient fortified mountaintop homes—one a working farm, the other a grander *palazzo*—bear witness to an age when bandits roamed the hills, and communities sought the protection of their overlord.

The Great Camp in the Adirondack Mountains was built for escape of a very different

sort. Its original owners were fleeing the social niceties of urban turn-of-the-century

life. Their wooden camp connected them with the pioneering spirit of their country.

Alpine chalets are perfectly designed for life on a mountainside. This newly built exam-

ple from Verbier in Switzerland has all the features that would have kept people and live-

stock safe and warm through the long winters, but none of the inconveniences. And

finally, there is the American house in Topanga Canyon near Los Angeles, an area known

for its wildfires. Protected by an advanced firefighting system and fireproof plastic coat-

ing, this must surely be the ultimate escape.

For each of these six homeowners, living perched on a mountain or hillside provides

the physical as well as the emotional escape they are seeking. There, high above the

valleys, they can revel in a very special enchantment, magic, and spirituality.

LEFT **By way of the "steps to heaven," the whole house has a sense of reaching to the sky. This type of spiritual architectural statement is found in all ages and cultures, from gothic arches to Eastern pagodas.**

Tepoztlán in Mexico is a magical place, and here the word magical is not used lightly. It must have been this magic that drew a certain Mexican workaholic sculptor there when he was looking for somewhere to build himself an escape from the noise and pollution of Mexico City.

For Tepoztlán is the site of one of three pyramids built on astrological principles six hundred years ago that form an equilateral triangle. It stands within sight of the great volcano Popocatépetl, in an area of volcanic mountains, where the copper deposits have long been thought to bring good health and healing dreams to the people living nearby. It is here that the sculptor came to add his dream, to build his retreat among the old indigenous community.

Although he has lived in many different countries and a wide variety of cities, and has traveled since he was a child, it was inevitable that the sculptor would eventually wish to return to his

STAIRWAY TO HEAVEN

Protected by the gods of the mountains and on the site of a six hundred-year-old pyramid, this sculptor's retreat has an aura of magic and healing.

Designed by a sculptor, the house seems to grow organically out of the land and is quite consciously connected to the earth and sky by the pathway and stairs leading up to the roof. Its star shape means that it is open to every aspect and every possible view—even to the distant Popocatépetl volcano. The result is an open pavilion that exists not just to contemplate nature, but also to pay homage to it.

Mexican roots. "People," he says, "can only be happy where they have emotional language. If, for example, you say 'blue' to a Mexican, he will see it differently to a Dane. You need the emotional language of your childhood."

To find a location that spoke the emotional language he understood, all he had to do was drive south from Mexico City. There, where the mountains rise starkly up from the valley and where Tepoztezo, the god of the wind, lives and reigns, he set about building his home. Tepoztlán is a small settlement, a place where the natives came to escape from the Spanish conquest and where there's long been a tradition of struggle for social rights. Motivated both by aesthetics and by his respect for the dignity of these people, he has now built a beautifully proportioned house covered in a reddish-brown paint made from sifted earth dug from the site and mixed with the sap of the *nopal* cactus. This is exactly the same mixture that the Mexicans of six hundred years before had used to paint their three pyramids.

Technically speaking, the building of the house posed enormous difficulties. First, there was the problem of water, or rather, the lack of it, for the site is like a desert for six months of the year. Then there was the problem of

THERE IS A SILENCE INTO WHICH
THE WORLD CANNOT INTRUDE.
THERE IS AN ANCIENT PEACE
YOU CARRY IN YOUR HEART

LEFT **The house plays host to the work of other artists. Here, a gift from a friend of a bleached wood sculpture graces the stump of a tree that has been struck by lightning.**
OPPOSITE **The view from the house is punctuated by a massive stone sculpture made by the Mexican artist Jorge Yazpik.**

OPPOSITE The path at the front of the house leads up to the angled doorway, shaped exactly like the floor-to-ceiling windows that look out on all sides. The end of the staircase, which stretches from ground to roof at the back of the house, can be seen rising above the front door. This repetition of architectural forms adds to the house's sense of calm. From the top of the staircase, there are magnificent views of the surrounding countryside.
LEFT To take advantage of the wonderful natural environment, the owners have created an outdoor dining pavilion, covered with thatched reed. From its shade, they enjoy the dramatic sunrises and sunsets over the mountains.
RIGHT A detail of the rough-hewn stone sculpture by Jorge Yazpik that stands on the path at the back of the house.

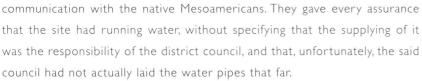

communication with the native Mesoamericans. They gave every assurance that the site had running water, without specifying that the supplying of it was the responsibility of the district council, and that, unfortunately, the said council had not actually laid the water pipes that far.

The water problem was not insuperable, but it made itself felt in the design of the house. The solution was to install a huge water cistern underneath, covered by a massive concrete floor. And, because the cistern needed to be connected to the water supply, the house then had to be built near the entrance to the site, not at its center, as originally planned.

It is hard to believe, but this complex retreat at Tepoztlán proves to be just a single room planned on the most stringent and minimal lines. But it is not a single room as we usually know it. Instead, we find ourselves in an eight-pointed star, designed so its huge floor-to-ceiling windows catch the light at any time of day, any season of the year.

Within the body of the star stand the bedroom, living room, dining room, and kitchen, each one basking in its own space, its own tranquility. And tucked away beneath the staircase that rises from yard to roof at the back of

ABOVE **In a space designed for one-room living, functionality is paramount. This transparent stairway designed by the owner can be moved around on its wheels to reach the storage areas over the bed/kitchen partition. Its design is based on a mathematical equation. The wooden sculpture is the artist's own work, and the upholstered chairs were bought in a New York flea market for their pleasing Art Deco shape.**

WE NEED TIME TO DREAM, TIME TO REMEMBER, AND TIME TO REACH THE INFINITE. TIME TO BE

the house, is the bathroom. Everything is there, and in its proper place. Nowhere does one feel the sort of overcrowding that often accompanies one-room living. Instead the star-shaped room exudes a sense of mystery and mysticism.

Outside, the magic continues. Here there is a staircase that starts in the yard at the back of the house and rises, enigmatically, not to a

OPPOSITE **From the path leading to the front door, one gets an impression of the whole light-flooded interior. The prominent deckchairs were found in New York. They come from a 1920s Cunard liner. The rest of the room is adorned with objects collected during the owner's travels in Africa. Behind the chairs hangs a length of African cloth and between them stands a small wooden table bought in Africa.**

OPPOSITE **One cozy angle of the room is dominated by the dining area. The table—a surprise gift—was designed by the Mexican metal-worker Juan Alvarez. The classic molded Philippe Starck chairs can also be used outside.**
RIGHT **This wall functions as a divider between kitchen and bedroom.**

second story, but to the roof. At first glance, it appears to have no purpose other than to provide a commanding view over the countryside. But its purpose is a spiritual one, for the staircase is not just a staircase, but a link between earth and sky. And the pathway that leads to the house at the front appears to join seamlessly with it so that staircase and pathway together make a single heavenward-pointing trajectory.

Peace, spirituality, and harmony with one's inner self are what this house is all about. Here, the owner and his partner have discovered the enormous, long-lost pleasure of solitude—"the gift of being with someone and yet alone—the gift of self! The moment when the exterior world

NO PERSON WHO IS NOT A GREAT SCULPTOR OR PAINTER CAN BE AN ARCHITECT. IF HE IS NOT A SCULPTOR OR PAINTER, HE CAN ONLY BE A BUILDER

is less important than the interior world. That is the gift that Tepoztlán gives us."

Here the sculptor feels he has re-established his oneness with the natural world, his understanding of the forebodings of the weather, his observation of animals, their agitation caused by the small earth tremors of the sleeping volcano warning them to beware. These are the connections that urban life so often and so sadly severs.

The design of the living space is based around the floor-to-ceiling paneled windows that slide back to give the impression of a Chinese garden house or pavilion. This feature is crucial to the concept of the house, providing its owner with a feeling of being out in the open. The windows can be shaded from the harsh Mexican sun by the banners of double-layered unbleached cotton that hang from hinged metal rods. As the house is of an unusual, if not unique, construction, such details had to be specially designed and commissioned.

Mandrascate looks as innocent as a hardworking old peasant who has led a virtuous life, tended his grapes, looked after his own, and danced at village weddings. But on closer inspection, the crenellated battlements, the ironwork grilles at the windows, and the embrasures—slits in the walls for firing through—reveal it to be a fortified *masseria*, or farmhouse.

Its seventeenth-century builder, Prince Pompeo Trigona, lived at a time when *banditi* regularly roamed the Sicilian countryside (a practice that continued right up until the nineteenth century) and when feudal lords such as he needed to be forever on the alert for the sudden bloodthirsty swoops of these brigands against their property, their people, and their livestock. In those days, the price of safety was eternal vigilance.

Mandrascate has now come down to a well-known Sicilian architect and his sisters from their great-grandfather, who inherited it in the nineteenth century. With love and affection, and with the great weight of family history on his shoulders, the architect now repairs and cares for the property, taking infinite pains that this country estate, which has always been so much in harmony with its natural surroundings, should remain that way.

In the olden days, the *padrone* of Mandrascate would live there only part-time. He and his family would visit for the harvest and perhaps grace the

farm with their presence through the summer. The semi-nomadic life they led, with servants and silver, dishes and bedlinen departing when they departed, is now a thing of the past, but the present owner, like his predecessors, is also a part-time resident. Yet

With its original thick stone-bastion walls, crenellations, embrasures, and ironwork grilles protecting its windows, the main courtyard, or *bagghiu*, of Mandrascate betrays the place's origins as a fortified farmhouse. In times of crisis, when local bandits would sweep through the countryside, families from the surrounding area would take refuge within Mandrascate's walls, bringing with them their livestock and crops. At other times, this courtyard would be their meeting place. There were, for instance, two bread ovens where local women could bring their bread to be baked. The two-storyed house, or *palazzotto padronale*, stands in this main courtyard, while other, smaller courtyards are surrounded by single-story agricultural buildings—still in use— and servants' quarters.

Masseria Mandrascate has stood, solid and strong, guarding its inhabitants against all foes for over three hundred years. Now its owner guards it from the encroachments of too much civilization.

IN THE MANDRASCATE MANNER

There is a strong sense of tradition in Sicily, and Mandrascate's present owner is intent on continuing the tradition of his *masseria* being a working farm. Thus rows of grapevines planted in the poor Sicilian soil flourish in the shadow of the old stone house and are tended just as in the days of the owner's forebears.

ALL REAL AND WHOLESOME ENJOYMENTS POSSIBLE TO MAN … TO WATCH THE CORN GROW, AND THE BLOSSOMS SET; TO DRAW HARD BREATH OVER PLOWSHARE OR SPADE; TO READ, TO THINK, TO LOVE, TO HOPE, TO PRAY—THESE ARE THE THINGS THAT MAKE MEN HAPPY

despite this and although he has a flourishing architect's practice and town house to maintain in Catania, he still takes an active interest in the running of Masseria Mandrascate.

For today, as in the past, Mandrascate is a working farm and, as was the case then, has to pay its way to survive. So its present owner can be found on the estate not only relaxing from the demands of his busy professional life, but also supervising the harvests of wheat, olives, and grapes at the appointed times of year.

The farmhouse was constructed in one go on foundations that were possibly dug in the six-teenth century. It is now perhaps one of the best-preserved examples of a seventeenth-century fortified farmhouse that Sicily has to offer.

Its buildings consist of a main courtyard or, in the local Sicilian dialect, *bagghiu*, in which stands the *padrone*'s two-story *palazzotto*, with his

Tall, rustic wooden ladders awaiting the olive harvest lean against the wall of one of Mandrascate's cavernous farm buildings. The stone-paved floor and wooden-beamed ceiling are typical of the traditional styles of construction used throughout the farm. The olives grown on the estate will be pressed there, and the oil stored in huge terracotta jars kept in one of the storerooms.

RIGHT The workers on the Mandrascate estate still produce a hearty wine from their grapes. After pressing and processing, the wine is poured into large old oak barrels that are stored in the perfect conditions of the deep, cool stone cellars. The third crop grown at Mandrascate is wheat. After the harvest, it is kept in the storerooms.

family's private accommodation on the upper floor. This type of central courtyard is typical of Italian farmhouses. Around the *bagghiu* are a number of other buildings that open onto smaller courtyards. Here are to be found the workshops, storerooms, haylofts, and servants' quarters that were all an essential part of the life of a working farm.

Fortunately for its current owner, Mandrascate was in a good state of repair when he inherited it, and most of the work that has been needed has

RIGHT Perched on its mountaintop, Mandrascate occupies a strategic site that looks down over the surrounding countryside. From here, with luck, marauding *banditi* could be spotted in time. Today, its solitary isolation makes it the perfect place to escape from civilization and to relax—at least when there's no pressing work to be done on the farm.

been conservation rather than restoration. The biggest job was to repair some of the flooring in the *palazzotto* using an ancient technique known as *coccio pesto*—literally "ground terracotta."

According to its current owner, Mandrascate was, in its heyday, the pivot around which a medieval style of feudalism revolved and, thanks to its location and imposing, complex architecture, has always been a point of reference for the agricultural life of the surrounding countryside. Indeed, many farmworking families once lived within Mandrascate's walls, enjoying the protection offered them by the *padrone* and his fearlessly constructed, valiant farmstead.

Thanks to the sensitivity of its architect-owner, a sense of continuity prevails at Mandrascate. The crops are planted, nurtured, and gathered just as they were three hundred years ago. The only difference is that, where once, without warning, the terrible cries of the *banditi* rang through the air, peace and serenity now reign.

LEFT AND RIGHT **The rooms of the *palazzotto* *padronale* are on a massive scale, but nowhere more than on the ground floor, used for receiving guests. Subject to a great deal of wear, the floors here were badly damaged and had to be restored using the *coccio pesto* technique— undamaged tiles were arranged in a grid and the remaining area filled with tinted cement and terracotta chips. Beneath a hanging display of plates stands a table constructed by the present owner from an old wooden door and a seventeenth-century base.**

THE HOUSE ... IS HIS CASTLE AND FORTRESS, AS WELL
FOR HIS DEFENCE AGAINST INJURY ... AS FOR HIS REPOSE

ABOVE AND RIGHT **The monastically simple combination of huge, airy, stone-vaulted, stone-paved rooms with furniture on a large scale, extends into the second floor of the *palazzotto*, where the** private apartments are located. Here, the occasional piece of elaborate furniture—the chandelier in the dining room and the unusual wooden plant stand— really leaps out.

WILD ADVENTURES IN THE ADIRONDACKS

As a child, the present owner of this magnificent stone and wood camp in the Adirondack Mountains had spent many a blissful summer in the region, walking, boating, picnicking. Yearning for a haven from her busy life in New York as a textile designer of international renown, she realized that such a haven existed in those mountains, along with her still-fresh childhood memories.

When a large part of one "great camp"—the main house, one of the boathouses, and the ice house—came on the market, she promptly bought it, complete with its length of shoreline, its turn-of-the-century decor, and its

Deep in the Adirondack Mountains, the owner of a Great Camp packed with hunting memorabilia and family heirlooms, carries on old traditions.

stuffed animal heads. The latter prompted one guest's son to comment, as only a child could, "Gee, you sure do have a lot of dead pets." Despite the dead pets, the camp, with its mountain backdrop and its stupendous views over the

Built in 1908 from stone and wood—traditional Adirondack building materials— the plot on which the main house of this "great camp" is found covers 1½ acres (half a hectare) and revels in 485 feet (14 meters) of Long Lake shoreline. Located in the northwest of the Adirondack Mountains, the least developed part, lake and house stand in wondrous forest—giant spruce, white pine, maples, silver birch.

lake, has proved the perfect place for the owner and her friends to find rest and relaxation.

This camp is relatively small, given the grandiose building schemes of the Vanderbilts and their ilk, who thought nothing of creating summer retreats of forty rooms or more. This Long Lake version has only thirteen rooms. In addition to these and the boathouse and ice house purchased by the present owner, the camp also included a laundry, a caretaker's cottage, a tennis court, a lean-to shed and a second boathouse. All in all, a modest undertaking!

It is not known who the camp was built for, apart from the fact that it was a family from the state of Maryland. Their annual trek from home, with their

OVER ALL THE MOUNTAINTOPS IS PEACE ... BIRDS IN THE FOREST ARE SILENT ... SOON, YOU, TOO, WILL HAVE PEACE

servants and their silver (summer life in the Adirondack Mountains was a quite grand affair for such people), would have taken two full days, some of it over rough terrain. Indeed, it was those very "robber barons"—the people who built the summer camps in the Adirondacks— who brought the railroad to upstate New York to

With vast areas of the Adirondacks to choose from, early pioneers could virtually pick their own lake or mountain to build a home. While some decided to build close to their friends, others followed the advice of clergyman William Henry Harrison Murray when he wrote, in 1864, in *Adventures in the Wilderness*, "You choose the locality which best suits your eye and build a lodge under unscarred trees, and upon a carpet of moss, untrampled by man or beast." Murray was credited with popularizing the area and causing a "stampede to the woods." In the early days, however, before the advent of the railroads, the only access to the camps was by water, so boats were an essential part of camp life. Today, with their old docks and boathouses, boats are still an important part of the escape, allowing modern escapees to feel something of the pioneering spirit.

ABOVE LEFT **The ice house has painted clapboard walls and a jaunty diamond-shaped window in its side extension. It is believed that this extension was added for a children's playroom.** ABOVE **The plentiful supply of wood in the Adirondacks made it one of the main building materials for the camps, as here, in the boathouse.**

ABOVE AND RIGHT **As the camps are solely for summer use, the covered porch is one of the most important rooms. Here, the owner-designer used the color taupe—her** signature color—to paint the tongue-and-groove paneling of the porch and its wicker furniture. The furniture is original to the house, but the gauze screens are replacements.

A MAN MUST KEEP A LITTLE
BACK SHOP WHERE HE CAN BE
HIMSELF WITHOUT RESERVE. IN
SOLITUDE ALONE CAN HE KNOW
TRUE FREEDOM

facilitate their summer migrations. That journey now takes between eight and nine hours, while the present owner can drive to the camp from either her home or her office in New York state in just about two and a half.

The main thing she did when she purchased the camp was to clean. Woodwork was washed and repainted, floors refinished, and appliances replaced. But the first owners would still recognize the house, with its Great Room, dining room, kitchen, butler's pantry, porch, bedroom, and bathroom on the ground floor, and its four bedrooms and two bathrooms upstairs.

Just a little furniture came with the house—including an unusual antler chandelier, which has become something of a talking point. Most of the rest is antique, much of it family pieces. The dining room table, for instance, has been in the owner's family for five generations.

On her many travels, she has bought a number of Asian antiques, and these, together with some modern designs, add interesting accents. Her eclectic decorating style manages, apparently effortlessly, to combine disparate objects to produce an understated, elegant look that people envy and which, using her own textile designs, she regularly recreates for her many clients.

The early days of the Adirondack camps included many formal events, the sort of occasion brilliantly described by American turn-of-the-century writers such as Henry James and Edith Wharton. Such was the nature of the East Coast establishment during the *belle époque*. The present owner loves to keep up those traditions

ABOVE AND BELOW
The camp's kitchen and bathrooms retain their original, calm simplicity, with natural wood flooring complemented by painted tongue-and-groove paneling. In the kitchen, plain country chairs are hung, Shakerlike, from a rail, while a bathroom is adorned with one of the house's many stuffed animal heads—a reminder of the days when the camp was a center for hunting, shooting, and fishing.

ABOVE LEFT **A quilt in the owner's signature taupe color and a pair of bronze stools in classical Greek style with woven leather seats bring a touch of elegance to the old pine wall paneling of the master bedroom.**

LEFT **In the Great Room,** taupe, used for the upholstery and the rug, again predominates, but instead of painting the pine paneling to match, the owner has left it natural. The original gallery leads to four bedrooms upstairs.

whenever she entertains. Visitors who stay for weekends are required to bring festive attire for the compulsory "dress-up" night, and birthday parties are evening-dress affairs. There are less formal occasions, too, such as lunch on the porch or dinner served on the dock by the lakeside. Being a designer, the owner pays enormous attention to the details that make a place special, and she loves to busy herself with every aspect of her guests' visits. In these respects, too, the original owners would probably recognize their old home. In their day, the mistress of the house would have run it with the same care and precision as the present mistress does.

In their day, too, despite the formality, Adirondack camp life was a life strictly regulated by nature. Then, as now, on the shores of Long Lake, toward the end of August, the evenings become cool, and the fires in the Great Room and the dining room have to be constantly maintained or it becomes impossible to heat the large building. Then, as now, the summer people gradually pack up their things and return to their everyday lives, while the great houses settle down to their winter slumber. Their owners are ready once again to face the onslaught of city life. Just as in the first days of the camps, the Adirondacks continue to weave their calming magic.

THE COUNTRY HABIT HAS ME BY THE HEART,
FOR HE'S BEWITCHED FOREVER WHO HAS SEEN,
NOT WITH HIS EYES BUT WITH HIS VISION, SPRING FLOW
DOWN THE WOODS AND STIPPLE LEAVES WITH SUN

ABOVE **The Great Room is a perfect 25-foot (7.5 meter) cube, heated by a massive fire. The granite fire surround, whose chimney extends well above the roof, radiates heat into the room. Other features include the many** mounted moose and deer heads and some lovely pieces of old family furniture. The wicker set is modern, but has an easy, gracious style that blends well with the room's original, turn-of-the-century features.

LEFT **As in many of the Great Camps, the dining room of this one leads off the Great Room. Like the Great Room, it is heated by a fireplace made from local granite. A set of chairs designed by Mies van der Rohe accompanies the family heirloom table, and a contemporary plexiglass and chrome light fixture hangs overhead. The sideboard is one of the few remaining pieces that came with the house. Originally painted bright blue, the owner's father refinished it, restoring it to a lovely warm honey color.**

MOUNTAIN RESCUE

Recycled lumber, a traditional design, and local wood carving create a feeling of great age in this comfortable family home in the Swiss Alps.

The owners of the yet-to-be-built house knew exactly what they wanted, and that was a traditional-style Swiss chalet full of light and shadowy corners, rich colors, old furniture, the smell of beeswax, and fine antique rugs. The chalet was to be an escape from their busy London life, and one of the requirements was that it include a library for quiet reading and contemplation.

The owners even knew exactly where they wanted their chalet, and that was in Verbier, in

BELOW The winter entrance to the chalet, leading to the "mud room," is in the stone-built ground floor, the part of the house that would have sheltered the animals. A wooden step ladder provides a means of reaching the second-floor balcony that can also be reached via the kitchen or the living room.

LEFT **A bench stands outside the chalet's summer entrance on the second floor, reached from above by stone steps or from below by a wooden staircase. In common with architectural styles in many parts of the world that suffer from long, cold winters, window areas have been kept to a minimum to help with insulation.**

Switzerland, a village they knew and had come to love from many family vacations spent there. They and their family had now outgrown the chalet they used to occupy. Something larger and more suited to their needs was now required.

Traditional Swiss chalets do not pop up on the market every day of the week, so to achieve what they wanted, they decided to build a new one, but using recycled, old lumber. Without further ado, the plot of land next to the oft-visited chalet

ABOVE **The chalet enjoys magnificent views of both the village and the mountains. Mindful of the beauty of the location, the owners added fifteen or so trees to the five or six that already stood on the site. In summer they let the grass grow wild around the house so they can enjoy the wealth of wild alpine flowers.**

was acquired, and a local architect was commissioned to draw up the plans. This venture was to be a maiden voyage for both architect and owners. He had never before been asked to produce a chalet-style house from traditional materials: they had never built a house from scratch.

The result is truly stunning—a family home with space for everyone and incorporating the longed-for library—with beautiful views over the village and the mountains, and with an age-old appearance that belies its recent construction.

This appearance is the fruit of much research. Although Verbier is now an attractive village, well and truly on the tourist trail, until twenty or thirty

WELL! SOME PEOPLE TALK OF MORALITY, AND SOME OF RELIGION, BUT GIVE ME A SNUG LITTLE PROPERTY

years ago, it was neither pretty nor prosperous. The farmhouses built here were on a rather modest scale and lacked any uniform style, unlike those in wealthier Swiss communities. So the architect turned to the two-hundred-or-so-year-old chalet style of the neighboring Val d'Iliez for his inspiration, and this beautiful home with its carved wood, low ceilings, small windows, and Val d'Iliez green shutters was born.

Traditionally, the ground floor of a Swiss chalet housed the animals, the second floor was for the humans, and the top floor, with its ventilation holes just under the steeply sloping eaves, was for the storage of the hay that provided food for the animals through the long winter months.

LEFT In the hall, a carved wooden staircase leads up to the main bedrooms and down to the children's rooms. The bench, with a backrest made of turned wooden spindles, has a seat cushion covered with striped Italian silk.
ABOVE AND RIGHT The dining room and living room occupy one large area on the second floor.

The long dining table is an old French piece, while the chairs are English chapel chairs. A built-in bench seat under the window provides additional seating. An open log fire dominates the living area, whose floor is covered with a richly colored kelim. The furniture here consists mainly of old French country pieces.

This new home retains that three-story construction, right down to the (unused) ventilation holes. Its ground floor, built from local stone, is the children's area, housing their bedrooms and bathrooms. In winter, the family uses an entrance on this level. Here there is a highly practical concrete-floored "mud room," where everyone can leave their muddy boots and skis.

The rest of the house is built of wood, with traditional carving carried out by craftsmen from nearby Val de Bagne. The summer entrance is on

FOLK ARCHITECTURE THAT APPEARS UNIFIED, HOMOGENOUS, EVEN IDENTICAL BECOMES, ON CLOSER INSPECTION, RICH, DIVERSIFIED, AND INDIVIDUALISTIC

ABOVE LEFT AND OPPOSITE In the master bedroom, the bed, covered by an antique quilt and with an old French cradle at its foot, nestles beneath the sloping eaves. Old French ticking makes bold pillow covers, while antique paisley is used for the curtains.
ABOVE AND LEFT The children's rooms have made-to-measure beds and closets, some of them painted with traditional Swiss country motifs. Accessories include horse blankets and bolsters.

ABOVE **The cozy feel of the chalet extends to the kitchen, with hand-painted wooden cabinets and Mexican tile behind the stove. Brass handles, woven baskets, a butcher's block, and copper pans continue the rustic theme.**

IT IS A FINE THING TO BE OUT ON THE HILLS ALONE. A MAN CAN HARDLY BE A BEAST OR A FOOL ALONE ON A GREAT MOUNTAIN

the second floor. Here are a brick-floored kitchen, the famous library, and a large all-in-one living/dining room, plus a huge balcony that wraps itself around one whole side and three-quarters of the front of the house, which can be reached from the kitchen or the living room. The master bedroom suite and two guest rooms are situated on the top floor, with a small balcony leading from the master bedroom. Overhanging it all are the wide eaves of the traditionally constructed wooden roof, providing shade for the balconies beneath when the sun reflects off the snow in winter or when it floods in during the glorious wildflower-studded summer months.

Unusually, the entire decorating scheme was worked out in London before the chalet was built. It was achieved using a model of the chalet-to-be, with flip-up sections giving a three-dimensional view of each room. The

interior decorator and the owner's wife scoured antique shops in London for suitable pieces of furniture, which were supplemented by pieces collected in Provence, some old, painted country furniture from Bohemia, and a number of pieces that were made to measure.

Now the work is finished, and the scent of wood smoke mingles with the aroma of ancient pine ceilings. The chalet glows with contentment. It looks like a building at least a century old.

ABOVE AND OPPOSITE BELOW **A table is set for a meal on the main balcony. Here, one can really appreciate the quality of the wood carving, while tremendous views over Verbier and the mountains make this a wonderful spot to sit, summer or winter.** RIGHT **A door opens onto the balcony in one corner of the kitchen.**

LEFT **With only an ancient horse trail and an obscure hiking path meandering past, it is easy to forget that Los Angeles is less then an hour away. At the housewarming party, guests were asked to scatter wild-flower seeds, so the house is now surrounded by sage, mustard, clover, poppies, lupines, yuccas, bachelor's buttons, and nasturtiums.** RIGHT **Space is not a problem in southern California, so the single-story plan was an affordable luxury. Four distinct modules, each a separate structure, nestle beneath the huge, barnlike steel roof. The building materials are functional, with construction-grade wood and structural steel used throughout, and often left exposed, as are the electricity conduits. Specially designed clamp-on lighting and polished concrete complete the residence's industrial feel.**

Peering out from beneath its sheltering roof, this plastic, concrete, and steel residence near Los Angeles is protected from the threat of wildfires.

FIREPROOF BY DESIGN

The house in Topanga Canyon, north of Los Angeles, was planned with escape of a very practical nature in mind. With summer temperatures frequently exceeding 100 degrees Fahrenheit (43 degrees Celsius) the area is regularly at the mercy of wildfires. This fact has driven the aesthetics of the design from the very beginning. The 43,000-square-foot (4,000-square meter) Palladian-style airport-hanger barn of a house,

The house is divided into four zones—the kitchen/family room, the living room/den, the children's rooms, and the bedroom suite—all connected by cross-axis hallways and converging beneath an atrium lit by an overhead skylight. This area, seen left and below, is used as a formal dining room. The loftlike living room features a twenty-foot (six-meter) span of fully retractable glass sliding doors that open the whole room to the landscape and the views beyond. But wherever you are in the house, the outside world is only a step away. Double doors from the central atrium on three of the axes lead straight out into the open, to sitting areas (right) shaded from the sun by the overhang of the roof.

HOUSES ARE BUILT TO LIVE IN AND NOT TO LOOK ON; THEREFORE LET USE BE PREFERRED BEFORE UNIFORMITY, EXCEPT WHERE BOTH MAY BE HAD

designed by architect Brian Murphy, is coated with plastic siding that will char in a fire, but not burn. In addition, the eaves are equipped with sprinklers which, if required, can create a fire-retardant curtain of water. Eventually, the house's block-wall plinth will be flooded, making the house appear to be floating in a lake. This will help cool the interior, but will also reflect light into the rooms deep inside and, most important, will serve, if required, as a backup reservoir for the water-sprinkler system.

Constructed from utilitarian materials—concrete, wood, aluminum, steel, and plastic—the house, with its novel series of four zones beneath a huge steel roof, is a temple to modernity—the perfect synthesis of beauty with practicality.

From the very earliest times, Castelluccio's hilltop site, overlooking the Mediterranean, would have played an important strategic role in this lawless and ruthless land. Indeed, neolithic remains—evidence of Sicily's first human inhabitants—were discovered here fifty years ago. Now gazing peacefully down on its orange, almond, and olive groves, its restored grounds are protected by sturdy baroque walls. The formal gardens near the house, with their tinkling fountains, little canals, pools, and stone benches, were designed in Andalusian style by the owners' friend and mentor, Teddy Millington-Drake.

SICILIAN CASTLE IN THE AIR

Escape has always been at the heart of this late-seventeenth-century Sicilian palazzo—then, escape from bandits, now, escape from modernity.

The idea of the Great Escape came, as if by stealth, to the owners of Castelluccio. They had arrived from Catania in eastern Sicily to spend a day amid the ruins of their seventeenth-century Sicilian palazzo when, gradually, inexorably, the dream was born to restore it to its former glory. Ancient, battered, ruined but staunch, Castelluccio—its name comes from the Latin *castrum*, meaning "camp"—was a legendary feudal domain dating from 1693. It sat, strategically, on top of a hill amid terraces of rough Mediterranean scrubland.

The decision to restore Castelluccio meant commitment on a grand scale for, obviously, it was not going to be restored in a day. But that commitment has been well rewarded. Its owner, who has always farmed the ancestral lands around Castelluccio from his home in Milan on the mainland, had a great sense of historical duty and an

ABOVE **Castelluccio's central two-story wing has its own church and tower with stunning views over the valley below.**
BELOW **A sense of history pervades Castelluccio. Here, at the end of a path leading to the belvedere, a statue of the Virgin Mary stands in place of the eighteenth-century gallows. The spot is now used as an outdoor "room" for family celebrations.**

LEFT **Old farm wagons, painted in traditional Sicilian style, await the harvest in one of the sheds. They are a reminder that Castelluccio is still a working farm.**
RIGHT **Local produce is served in the courtyard.**

buildings, while others have been converted into guest accommodation. Part of the upper story of the main building has been transformed into still more guest rooms.

Under Millington-Drake's guidance, the early nineteenth-century additions to the main building were removed, and this part of the palazzo completely restored to its former glory. Though, sadly, Millington-Drake died before the work was completed, his disciples have remained faithful to his ideals and inspiration.

Together they had a vision of a restoration where there would be not a hint of pomp or circumstance. Any ostentatious elegance would be

enormous helping of zeal. That, combined with the determination, sense of style, and imagination of his fashion-designer wife, has made Castelluccio the spellbinding place it is today.

And, during the cold winter months, when they were perhaps beginning to lose heart, it was the owners' old friend, the talented artist and interior decorator, Teddy Millington-Drake, who gave them the final push and the vision of the majestic simplicity of the finished work.

To understand the scale of Castelluccio, one must remember that it was once a great feudal center, a place where all human life unrolled. It had its own well, a church, and, in the eighteenth century, a gallows—sited in the belvedere. Thankfully, the gallows have been replaced by a statue of the Virgin Mary, and the spot is now a focus for pious pilgrimage rather than for bloody punishment.

The palazzo consists of a two-story central wing, an inner courtyard, and a cluster of secondary buildings—including a tower with breathtaking views over the grounds—some of which serve their original purpose as farm

RIGHT **A local painted nineteenth-century bench and massive olive jars were saved from decay and now stand in a cool room off the central courtyard.**
OPPOSITE **The converted stables house a Moorish-style lounging and changing area. From the raised, mattress-strewn divans, one has a captivating view of the swimming pool with its own cooking area and dining table shaded by a shrub-covered arbor.**

I AM I PLUS MY SURROUNDINGS, AND IF I DO NOT PRESERVE THE LATTER, I DO NOT PRESERVE MYSELF

LEFT AND ABOVE **Although Castelluccio was extensively restored, it still retains its sense of age. From the peeling exterior walls to the original shelves in the second-floor pantry, colors and textures were assiduously recreated. In the pantry the cheese is stored in a suspended glass case. Fruit, vegetables, and wine all come from the estate.**

quite out of tune with the simple life that had been lived there for generation on generation. Grand though the place may have been in concept, it was still a testament to lives lived under the harsh Sicilian sun, to ruined harvests and to Roman, Norman, and Bourbon domination.

Simplicity and sensitivity to Castelluccio's Sicilian origins are the keynotes to the restoration. When the present owner inherited the house from his old aunt, almost all the valuable objects and furniture had been sold and what remained were the simpler country pieces. Fortunately, these suited the owners' vision perfectly.

Another factor that was to play a part in the refurbishment of Castelluccio was its relative inaccessibility. This forced the owners to source as much as possible from local craftsmen and markets. Thus, the dining chairs are simple, painted pieces made by a local carpenter, while traditional crisp white Sicilian drawn-threadwork

RIGHT **The color of the nineteenth-century hutch in the breakfast room is original, as is the gilt lettering on its doors. The vase on the table is Italian faïence from Caltagironi.** ABOVE RIGHT **The cool colors in the dining room were chosen by the owners, but proved identical to previously used colors that were found under old wallpaper. The porcelain in this room is one of the house's few remaining antiques. It is by Ginori and bears the crest of the Marchese de Castelluccio.** FAR RIGHT **The lilac guest bedroom opens off the breakfast room. It has a late-eighteenth-century iron bedstead and a hand-embroidered curtain bought locally.**

SHOW ME A MAN WHO CARES NO MORE FOR ONE PLACE THAN ANOTHER, AND I WILL SHOW YOU IN THAT SAME PERSON ONE WHO LOVES NOTHING BUT HIMSELF. BEWARE OF THOSE WHO ARE HOMELESS BY CHOICE

cloths decorate the hutch and a table in the dining room. A nineteenth-century hand-embroidered curtain found in a local market graces the window of one of the guest bedrooms and is complemented by an iron bed, also found locally, dating from the eighteenth century. Locally bought fabric has also been used for the upholstery in the living room.

Castelluccio's grounds are another of its treasures. Two formal gardens enclosed by baroque walls and in Moorish style—inspired by a visit the owners made to Andalusia—lead to a stone swimming pool, which, in turn, gives onto a garden with planting in the style of the early twentieth-century English garden designer Gertrude Jekyll. Beyond this "wild" garden lie the ever-present mauve-gray Sicilian mountains.

The grand-scale commitment undertaken by the owners continues unabated. There is always work to be done—the restoration of the church is the current project—and, because of their determination to employ only original building techniques, that work progresses slowly. But the satisfaction it brings to the owners when they arrive from Milan and see their beautiful hilltop property and its farmlands, knows no bounds.

A MAN TRAVELS THE WORLD OVER IN SEARCH OF WHAT HE NEEDS AND RETURNS HOME TO FIND IT

In the bedrooms and bathrooms, an unpretentious style prevails. There is a hint of grandeur in the four-poster bed, but a closet is nothing more than a curtained-off corner. The chairs, beds, and benches were made by Sicilian craftsmen, as was the marble tub in the alcove, filling a space where a bed once stood. Local styles were used for most of the new pieces, but some were copied from Millington-Drake's house on the Greek island of Patmos. The two Mediterranean island styles mix well.

WOODLAND ESCAPES

Living in woodland is to live with a sense of security that other natural locations do not always provide. No matter that, in most parts of the world, woodlands are also home to menacing animals, the sheer physical presence of the canopy of leaves and branches overhead and the soft leafmold or pine needles underfoot creates a protective envelope into which we can comfortably slip, relax, and dream.

In woodland, the changing seasons are constantly present. In wintertime the mood is often dark and chilled, the trees starkly bare or immutably green, and the air crisply biting. Spring brings a gentle warmth as buds burst and the woodland floor rustles to the movement of small creatures and plants venturing out after the winter. Summertime patterns of dappled light and shade on the ground are strikingly haunting and ephemeral, while the colors of the autumn leaves appear capriciously mutable. Then, as winter approaches once more, the still-warm air starts to fill with the cloying scent of decay.

Each owner of the four houses featured here was adamant that his or her perfect escape from the rigors and demands of modern living lay in a woodland clearing, whether natural or artificial. Our first visit is to a restored turn-of-the-century water tower that stands in a wooded glade not far outside Antwerp in Belgium. Its owner believes his woodland setting to be so exquisitely perfect that he has no need of decoration inside his home, just of huge picture windows that allow the woodland spirit into every room. By contrast, outside Malibu in California, a top fashion model nurtures her tropical garden through willful neglect. Its enormous shrubs and trees—even its wildlife—create a forestlike presence wherever you turn. Still in the United States, an eighteenth-century house in Litchfield, Connecticut, nestles in the woods, its original clapboard covering and broad wooden floorboards a reminder of the infant days of the American nation when buildings were made from whatever was at hand. Finally, we are guests at a collection of wooden farm buildings in the ancient forests near the Delaware River. Here, frenetic urban life quickly slows to a gentler pace as the woodland setting casts its spell over all who visit.

Whereas, since time began, humans on every continent have plundered woods and forests, here are four people who appreciate the spiritual calm that peaceful coexistence can bring. The trick for each has been to find a balance between modern comfort and the simple woodland life. They have all succeeded beyond their wildest dreams.

EYRIE IN ANTWERP

Shimmering in the evening light of winter, a once-condemned six-story former water tower stands like a glass sentinel in a wooded Belgian glade.

For many years there had been talk of knocking down the unused water tower in the wooded copse in Brasschaat outside Antwerp. It might have been the first concrete-built water tower in Belgium, with excellent temperature control to make sure that the ground floor was warm and sheltered in winter, and cool and sheltered in summer, but what was the good of that?

But then a local landscape architect appeared on the scene. He had known for many years of the strange tower in the woods with a river running by and had dreamed of what it might be like to live in it. Being something of a visionary, he bought the weird structure—it was really nothing more than a huge barrel with a concrete pump room nestling between its skeletal legs—from the municipality, who eventually granted him permission to change its use.

It took two arduous years to create a concrete and glass outer skin, specially constructed to stand separate from the original building. During that time, whenever the architect-owner felt low and nothing much seemed to be happening, he held firm to the dictum of Tadao Ando, the "new wave" Japanese architect of the late twentieth century: "Architecture should bring calm in a world increasingly tainted by consumerism." This was the calm he was looking for, and with the help of an architect colleague, it was a calm he was finally to attain.

A water tower, clearly, is never going to be a conventional home. This one has, of course, the

In its previous incarnation as a skeletal water tower, this unusual structure had been earmarked for demolition. Built between 1900 and 1910 by the owner of a castle in Brasschaat to provide a private source of water, it held two thousand gallons (a hundred cubic meters) of water. This was taken from the river, filtered, and pumped up to the reservoir via the concrete "box" on the ground floor—the pump room. In 1937, castle and houses were provided with city water so the tower fell into disuse. In 1950, the municipal government of Brasschaat bought the castle with its park and water tower, but didn't know what to do with the tower. The present owner, who worked for the government, has brought it back to life.

elements of such a home, but here they are stacked on top of one another so they make the visitor gasp at the sheer audacity of it all.

The layers seem to go on forever. Beneath the ground and accessed through a massive, aluminum, counterbalanced hatch, there's an enormous cellar used for storage and wine. Above that, the double-height concrete base—the original pump room—has had holes punched through it to make the huge windows that give wonderful views of the woods and river. This ground floor has now become the kitchen and

Dominated by a white plastic-covered sofa, the ground floor of the water tower now houses the kitchen and living areas. The restoration of the tower was governed by the owner's desire to have as much of the original structure as possible on view, hence the massive concrete beams. The huge new windows, triple glazed on this floor for insulation, provide breathtaking views of the small wooded glade and its river. The impression is almost one of looking out from a moated manor house. The distinctly industrial atmosphere on this level, enhanced by the rough gray concrete walls and the minimal furniture, is deliberate. The owner feels that all the richness he needs comes from the space outside, viewed through the great expanses of glass.

living areas, one vast, open expanse, scarcely broken up by the great, raw concrete beams and pillars of the new construction. Think of a space that would be excellent for parties, and this one would fit the bill. The owner, being something of a party animal, takes full advantage of it.

By contrast, the second-floor rooms, situated in the light, ethereal glass tower, are smaller and more intimate, with a bathroom and shower room, and a tiny TV/music room. Here, the use of wood gives a warmer, cozier atmosphere, almost, the owner says, like being in a ship's cabin.

EVERY MAN'S WORK, WHETHER IT BE LITERATURE OR MUSIC OR PICTURES OR ARCHITECTURE OR ANYTHING ELSE, IS ALWAYS A PORTRAIT OF HIMSELF

ABOVE **Adjoining the wood-paneled TV room on the second floor is a shower room and this bathroom, whose very functionalism is a source of delight to the owner. The color blue, in the shape of a mass of small mosaic tiles, has been introduced in the bathroom in deference to the tower's original use as a water reservoir. A round skylight highlights the rough concrete finish of the walls and allows the owner to sit in the bathtub and gaze at the sky and tower above.**
FAR RIGHT **On the third floor, the owner has built his own bed in a room designed to give the feeling that the bed is floating among the trees. Sandblasted glass on one side provides some privacy.**
RIGHT **Steep aluminum steps lead up from the bedroom to the office. Working here for a month one summer on a thesis, the owner enjoyed the feeling that this room provided of being completely in touch with the outside environment.**

Above the ship's cabin, it's a short winding aluminum step to the main bedroom. Standing in solitary splendor and with amazing views from all sides, this occupies the entire floor. Here, where there is no central heating—the heating stops at the second floor—the bed is surrounded by floor-length white curtains to help keep out the drafts at night. Wooden bed and headboard are one, the headboard being nothing more than a stack of bookshelves to hold the owner's beloved collection of books.

and everything inside was to have a clear relationship with the environment outside.

So he decided to build most of the furniture himself, or to have it specially made. Each item was to have its own history, its individual stamp. The local woodland would provide the beautifully figured hawthorn wood used for the kitchen surfaces, while the cherry wood for the large table in the living area would come from a local tree. The warmth and texture of these woods would provide a striking contrast with the concrete, glass, and aluminum that are at the heart of the building's structure.

So now the turn-of-the-century water tower that stands in the glade in Brasschaat outside Antwerp has been given a new purpose in life. Where once the seasons unfolded, observed only by the woodland birds and animals, now they form the backdrop to a spacious, inspired retreat whose owner has found peace and calm, and a place where he can be at one with nature.

THE WOODS ARE LOVELY, DARK AND DEEP, BUT I HAVE PROMISES TO KEEP, AND MILES TO GO BEFORE I SLEEP

Onward and upward to the office on the next floor, followed by the guest bedroom on the next, and—we've now arrived at the top floor—the winter garden, overflowing with pittosporum plants brought back from France. They fill the room with their glossy, evergreen forms, providing a sense of life when everything outside in the woods is brown, gnarled, and leafless.

Then above that—a sort of seventh floor—rises the water reservoir—the tower's original *raison d'être*. The owner plans that one day this may become a swimming pool.

To maintain a sense of connection with the original simplicity of the water tower, the owner decided that the reconstructed building would be as minimal as possible, and that minimalism would rule on the inside as well. With sky and trees and distant city spires to feast the eye, he felt there was no need for decorative distractions inside. Nothing was to go into the building that didn't have a very good reason for being there

The house in the chaparral-covered hills outside Malibu belonging to the top fashion model is still not complete, but that's how she likes it. She prefers things to be evolving rather than to reach a conclusion because, as she says, if you bring things to a conclusion, what else can happen?

Her house is still happening. Transported from its former life of shiny brass and pink marble, in a style that was absolutely *not* to her taste, it's now a hippy, easy-come-easy-go sort of place. She leads a frenetic life all over the world, but is a great animal-lover, a vegetarian, and a respecter of the

SPIRIT DWELLING PLACE

With its air of meditative spirituality, this hillside house is a sanctuary for humans and animals alike.

Surrounded by a high fence to keep out the coyotes, the jungle-like garden is central to the house and to the owner's lifestyle. Rampant vegetation seems on the point of invading everything, inside and out.

Once owned by a nurseryman, the yard was already full of plants when its present owner acquired it. The enveloping morning fogs provide the perfect environment for the tropical and semi-tropical plants that have now been added. A rough concrete path leads past salvaged patio furniture to the front door, while brick paving surrounds an old fountain embellished with new mosaic.

LEFT Steel-framed glass doors lead out onto a balcony from the master bedroom, helping to blur the distinction between indoors and out.
BELOW More large windows in the kitchen make it feel as if the luxuriant garden is encroaching even here.
BELOW LEFT AND RIGHT Steps lead down from the front door to the "music room," and this, in turn, leads into the dining room and out into the yard. The owner is passionate about recycling, so the staircase was made from old ironwood, charred black from the Malibu fires that raged in the region in the early 1990s. Pieces of fossilized shell, once embedded in the hillside, decorate the stair risers.

SILENCE IS AS FULL OF POTENTIAL WISDOM AND WIT AS THE UNHEWN MARBLE OF GREAT SCULPTURE

environment, so she was searching for somewhere that would feel at one with the natural world. With the help of the New York architect and designer Jeffrey Cayle, and in the space of only about ten months, from conception to moving in, that is exactly what she has found.

Cayle retained the exterior structure of the early 1970s house, but he opened it up to the

LEFT AND RIGHT **The owner is not a collector of things and had few possessions of sentimental value, so the architect took care to introduce only items that were interesting on account of their color, texture, or the story they told. The master bedroom is decorated with a relaxed mixture of objects that meet these criteria.**

outside by adding plenty of large, steel-framed windows. The spacious sunken "music room" is now the heart of the house, where all her friends gather. Leading off it are the dining room and kitchen with terrific views over and access to the luxuriant yard, and from the kitchen you reach the "womb room," a deep, dark, cozy sanctuary dominated by a fireplace carved from rock and a huge television set. A covered walkway leads to an office and a guest room. Upstairs is the master bedroom, the "meditation room," and, with stunning views over the yard below, a bamboo and plant-lined bathroom.

The yard is unforgettable. Here, Cayle has adapted the small stream that ran through it, so instead of drying up for part of the year, it is constantly fed with recycled water from a pond at the bottom of the hill. Amid the chaotic, overgrown tropical and subtropical plants that flourish in the grounds—the owner can never bear to remove any plant, even if it's dead—somewhere, if you can find them, are the stables, home to her beloved white horse.

Meanwhile, in the house's cool interior, with fans whirring softly from immensely high ceilings, her many pets—dogs, cats, a cockatoo, even the horse—are allowed to wander through at will, accompanying their lovely exotic mistress as she pads barefoot through one room after the other. They, like her, see no difference between inside and outside. For them, her unfinished sanctuary is not just an escape, it is a lair.

THE SOUL OF A HOUSE, THE ATMOSPHERE ... ARE AS MUCH A PART OF THE HOUSE AS THE ARCHITECTURE

ABOVE **The owner wanted a meditation area, and this quiet upstairs room proved to be the ideal spot. The floorboards were left natural, the walls painted white, and a cotton hammock was slung from wall to wall. When the owner is in residence, she uses the room for an hour every morning.**

LEFT **Overlooking the yard and with its walls clad in bamboo stems and living plants, the bathroom feels like an outdoor space. The hand-molded rough cement bathtub is decorated with shells.**

Nestled in the woods on the outskirts of Litchfield, Connecticut, a restored clapboard-covered house takes its place in American history.

INDEPENDENT SPIRIT

Oliver Wolcott's eighteenth-century house now sits on a 14-acre (5½-hectare) wooded site. When the town of Litchfield was laid out in 1717, its planners deemed this size appropriate to a "townhouse building plot." The house's front door is original. The portico was added around 1790 and its gilded fanlight is said to represent the "rising sun" of the American nation. The yard is an interpretation of its nineteenth-century predecessor. "Skeletal" elements of the older yard have been found.

In the orchard behind the house, while the American War of Independence was raging, the women and children of Litchfield melted down a statue of King George III to make bullets to use against the British soldiers.

The house had been built in 1754 for Oliver Wolcott, Sr. then Colonial High Sheriff of Litchfield, Connecticut. Wolcott was later to be one of the signatories to the Declaration of Independence, and in 1780, and again in 1781, his home was to play host to George Washington. The ideals to which Wolcott had devoted his life were enshrined in that Declaration, and he died, a happy man, in the house he built, in 1797.

With the passing of the years, the house, with its typical colonial "center chimney" hall and massive chimney stack, fell into disrepair. It was in a sorry state when it came into the hands of its present owners, the chairman of a private investment firm in New York and his interior-designer wife.

For them, it was the vacation home they were looking for, but it was not just a house, but a place of pilgrimage, and as such it deserved to be restored with respect. Their labor of love has resulted in an edifice that is not only a

ABOVE AND RIGHT
The Keeping or Long
Room retains its original
wide oak floorboards and
virgin "old growth" pine
paneling below the dado
rail, but the paneling above
the fireplace is a
reconstruction. The
American colonies were
not allowed a glass
industry, so the window-
panes in the room are
made from the largest size
of glass that could be
imported from England.
It was a size that stowed
easily in a ship's hold. The
room has a fine
seventeenth-century
English oak gateleg table
and an eighteenth-century
fishing-rod rack to go with
the two oil paintings of
fish. The nineteenth-
century candle chandelier
is wrought iron.

BELOW The library is
furnished with an
assortment of country
furniture, while the oil
painting, "Niagara Falls," is
an American work dated
around 1840–60.

OPPOSITE The paneling in
the dining room dates
from the building of the
house, but the windows
were "modernized" in
about 1888 with the
addition of larger panes.

GOD HAS GIVEN US VAST FORESTS, IMMENSE FIELDS, WIDE HORIZONS; SURELY WE OUGHT TO BE GIANTS, LIVING IN SUCH A COUNTRY AS THIS

shrine to democracy, but also a comfortable and beautiful New England home.

Not surprisingly, the house has been extended over the years. A two-story south wing was added in the eighteenth century, a barrel porch containing the original front-door pediment arrived at the beginning of the nineteenth, an east-wing kitchen came in the second half of the nineteenth century, closely followed by a turret, and the century came to a close with the addition of a third story for the south wing—the so-called ballroom—with a number of window seats set beneath leaded-glass windows.

But despite these additions, the house retains the character and atmosphere of a classic colonial home. This is thanks to the present owners, for whom it was essential that the restoration be carried out accurately and sympathetically. To help them in their endeavor, they enlisted an expert from the Society for the Preservation of New

WE LIVE IN A HISTORIC LANDMARK … PERHAPS WE ARE SIMILAR TO A CHIPMUNK FORTUNATE ENOUGH TO LIVE IN A GRAND OAK TREE. ONE CAN FEEL PLEASED AND PROUD OF IT WITHOUT CLAIMING CREDIT

England Architecture, who carried out a paint analysis, thus insuring that the paint colors used were authentic. In addition, they employed a firm of woodwork and plaster restorers who adhered strictly to eighteenth-century techniques. The result is a home that is simple and cozy but stylish, just as would have befitted the high-minded gentleman and soldier who built it.

Original, hand-routed, beaded clapboards protect the house's exterior, and the wide floorboards of the second floor are still held in place with the original, handmade nails, but the highlight of Wolcott's house must surely be

THE SECOND DAY OF JULY 1776 WILL BE THE MOST
MEMORABLE EPOCH IN THE HISTORY OF AMERICA ...

the Keeping, or Long Room. This room, with its cooking fire and its original "12 over 12" windows, would have been at the heart of Wolcott's home. Now it houses a number of his letters and some early etchings. It is also home to the discreet brass plaque that designates the house a

National Historic Landmark, an honor granted thanks to the purity of the house's architecture and detail, and to its having been built by a Signatory to the Declaration of Independence. Only two or three such plaques are in private homes in Connecticut. The owners of Wolcott's house are justly proud of having one of them in theirs.

But they also take pride in the way they have recreated a small part of the most glorious period of American history. Their recreation has given them an escape from the technology-obsessed twentieth century to a more gracious, leisurely age, when ordinary men could still accomplish great things.

OPPOSITE TOP LEFT
This corner cabinet was added to the dining room in about 1790 as part of the decorations carried out by Wolcott to celebrate America's independence from England. The wainscoting dates from 1754, when the house was built.
OPPOSITE BELOW LEFT
The fine staircase, dating from about 1770, when "center hall" architecture came to Litchfield, leads to the five bedrooms on the second floor. The chimney from the Keeping Room fireplace ran behind the staircase wall. The paint is the original color—a glaze of gray-green over yellow. In about 1820, all the houses in Litchfield were painted a fashionable off-white, and it was only by chemical analysis that the original paint colors were discovered.
OPPOSITE ABOVE AND
RIGHT **The bedrooms have all been decorated in a lighter, early nineteenth-century style.**
LEFT **A freestanding bathtub with claw feet stands in the center of the 1920s-style bathroom. Plumbing would have been introduced to the house in the nineteenth century.**

WOODLAND HIDEAWAY

Deep in the ancient forests near the Delaware River, a collection of wooden farm buildings makes the perfect escape from modernity. Mildred's House, the Horse Shed, the Barn, the Guest Tent, and four artistic spirits—each has a story to tell.

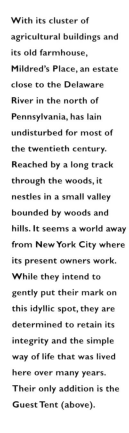

With its cluster of agricultural buildings and its old farmhouse, Mildred's Place, an estate close to the Delaware River in the north of Pennsylvania, has lain undisturbed for most of the twentieth century. Reached by a long track through the woods, it nestles in a small valley bounded by woods and hills. It seems a world away from New York City where its present owners work. While they intend to gently put their mark on this idyllic spot, they are determined to retain its integrity and the simple way of life that was lived here over many years. Their only addition is the Guest Tent (above).

For over eighty years, since she had been brought there as a baby by her parents, a fine old lady called Mildred lived on the ninety-acre (thirty-six-hectare) estate in northern Pennsylvania near the Delaware River. There was no electricity, and she drew water from a natural spring.

In summer she flourished in the warm sunshine; in the fall, she cooked up the fruits of the harvest; in winter, the cold weather only slightly hampered her activities, and come spring, she was up and ready to confront the occasional coyote and black bear if necessary.

Mildred was one of that happy breed of privileged human beings who are completely at home in the natural world. Here, on the estate, was an escape, and Mildred was well aware of it.

When the time came, there was a new generation of escapees waiting in the wings. They were a clothes designer and her partner, an entomologist

ABOVE The second-floor veranda attached to Mildred's House seems to lean precariously into the valley, so that a table's front legs have to be propped up on bricks. All the original paintwork is in the muted colors typical of the late nineteenth century. Sitting in Mildred's old rocking chair and looking out over the gently undulating countryside, the new owners can enjoy the sense of timelessness that Mildred's Place offers.

and world-famous conceptual artist. This sophisticated pair worked and earned a living in New York, but yearned for the simple life and an escape from the stressful life of that city.

Mildred's Place, set in woodland amid rolling countryside, suited them perfectly. It was within reach of New York, so they could spend weekends and vacations in Pennsylvania, yet could easily travel back to New York. But, above all, Mildred's Place embodied humility and solid values, and this was part of what they were seeking. They were good and ready to throw in their lot with the black bears.

RIGHT The canvas wallcovering downstairs in Mildred's House was installed to provide some insulation. It is the only room in the house to have it. Painted vibrant blue in the early twentieth century, the present owners have refrained from repainting it. The contrasting strips of wood keep the canvas in place, but are also decorative. Mildred would still feel at home here, among her furniture.

LEFT **The Red Hut**—the outdoor privy—sits where it always has, behind Mildred's House. Despite its down-to-earth function, it has always been attractively decorated, inside and out.

RIGHT **An old collection of model boats stands above an unused fireplace in Mildred's House.**

FAR RIGHT **The Horse Shed makes a comfortably furnished, candlelit home.**

The designer-owner is a true original. Hailing from a small town (population 1,000) in Georgia, she has a soul that is truly rural. Her New York premises boast a concrete mixer in the middle of the floor, and her family motto is, appropriately, "As long as you're green you grow, but when you think you're ripe, you begin to rot."

This motto has probably whetted her enthusiasm to make Mildred's Place a living organism

IN THE UNITED STATES THERE IS MORE SPACE WHERE NOBODY IS THAN WHERE ANYBODY IS. THAT IS WHAT MAKES AMERICA WHAT IT IS

rather than just a weekend place for tired urban-ites. The search for somewhere that was more than a chichi bolthole was what also led two artist friends of hers to join in this really big farm adventure. Together, the four constitute a reso-lutely spirited pioneering band.

Since they arrived, they have made some changes, but, apart from converting the unused agricultural buildings into basic dwellings for human habitation—they charmingly call it "adaptive re-use"—their changes are relatively superficial. Their aim is to make Mildred's Place habitable, but to leave as much as possible alone.

IN THOSE VERNAL SEASONS OF THE YEAR, WHEN THE AIR IS CALM AND PLEASANT, IT WERE AN INJURY … AGAINST NATURE NOT TO GO OUT, AND SEE HER RICHES, AND PARTAKE IN HER REJOICING WITH HEAVEN AND EARTH

The Horse Shed, with its new pine siding, deep-buttoned sofa, and fruitwood rocker, is where the designer likes to sketch, drink her morning coffee, and make business calls. One side is open, screened from the summer sun by a simple, looped-up canvas awning. An old washstand and basin are the only washing facilities here.

Though Mildred drew her water from a spring and stored it in jars in a sort of cave under the house, the new owners have drilled a well. They have also installed electricity in some parts of the house. Despite these changes, the spirit of the house remains as true and steady as ever.

With the house came the furniture. Where restoration was needed, it was kept to a mini-mum, and any additional furniture consists either of old pieces inherited by the designer, or objects found in flea markets or junk stores. As far as

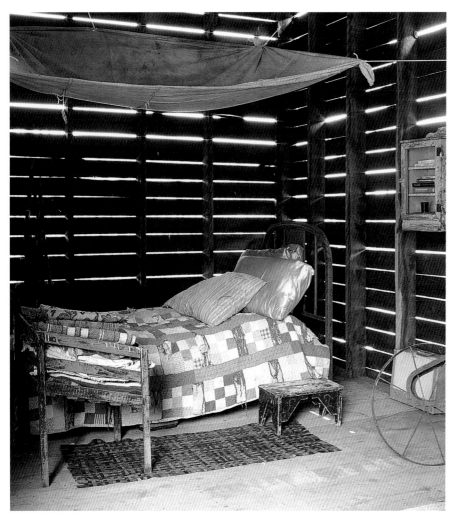

possible, the present-day owners want to feel as if they are gently shuffling in Mildred's footsteps.

The Horse Shed, converted from a stable, is the place where the designer and her partner sleep and relax. It has no electricity, but has been covered with new pine boards, each one—in true Mildred spirit—sawn and nailed in place by the designer with her own hands.

The late-nineteenth-century two-rooms-up two-down farmhouse—the building known as Mildred's House—has been left much as it was, with its original eccentric canvas wallcovering and its gaudy paintwork. Downstairs is gradually being transformed into a library of books on art, history, philosophy, design, and natural history—subjects that reflect the interests, the obsessions even, of the four inhabitants. In due course, when its restoration is complete, the designer and her partner hope to move in.

Wishing to stay true to Mildred's spirit, they have decided to preserve the Red Hut just as it was in Mildred's time. It was then, and continues to be,

ABOVE **One of the beds now standing in the Barn was found elsewhere on the property, while the quilt and other fabrics were found in the owner's grandmother's attic in Georgia. The wooden slats of the walls and roof keep off most of the rain, but a piece of tarpaulin strung over the bed has been added as a precaution.**

FOLK DESIGN METHOD [IS] ONE OF THE MOST PERVASIVE AND WELL-CONCEIVED DESIGN METHODS IN THE HISTORY OF CIVILIZATION

ABOVE **The Barn's sitting area is protected from the elements by another canvas tarpaulin. The painted trunk was found, full of old family letters, in the chicken coop.**
LEFT **Indoor dining takes place only in bad weather.**

the privy, its interior painted green and pink, its floor adorned with floral linoleum, and its windows screened with fresh lace curtains.

The large, airy, wood-slatted Barn, once used for storing straw and hay for the animals and grain for the humans and chickens, has now been taken over by the two artists, who have built a two-story wooden structure in its center. It does not get any natural light, but it does provide them with a bedroom above and a reading room below. The rest of the Barn is where the four

THE CARES THAT INFEST THE DAY SHALL FOLD THEIR TENTS LIKE THE ARABS, AND … SILENTLY STEAL AWAY

inhabitants get together to sit, cook, and eat.

In this part of the property, perhaps more than anywhere else, the residents' needs come second to those of the building and the environment. Evidence of this is the fact that the Barn is not completely waterproof, nor is it proof against bird and animal droppings. It also lacks electricity, but it would be anathema to the new owners to have electricity installed, or to close up the gaps between the wooden slats of the walls and roof. Instead, they make do, reading and going to bed by candlelight and stringing protective tarpaulins above vulnerable sitting and sleeping areas. The Barn may now be a dwelling, but its owners celebrate rather than try to disguise its agricultural origins.

The only new structure on the estate, if it can be called a structure, is the Guest Tent. As its name suggests, this is the place where weekend visitors stay. The bed that now graces it was found at the top of Mildred's House and brought down, in triumph. The Guest Tent backs onto the woods. It requires a guest of a certain mettle to lie in Mildred's old bed, listening to the cries of the coyotes and wondering if, by chance, there's going to be a visit from a big, black bear.

For the four owners, Mildred's Place is the escape route into the existence they would all be living had urban life and economic reality not intruded. Because the other three travel a great deal, the designer is the linchpin of the whole undertaking. She spends the most time there and has now almost completely turned her back on New York. Her metropolitan home has been sold. Once-a-week visits to the Big Apple are more than enough for this woman with the rural soul.

The Guest Tent has been created with the nomad in mind. Even its furniture has led a nomadic life, much of it having started out in Mildred's House. The crib is a tree-crib, the sort that farmers' wives would hang from the trees as they worked in the fields. Lying awake in the Guest Tent, one can hear the sound of rain dripping onto the canvas from the surrounding hemlock, white pine, and ash trees. As the American writer Thomas W. Dewing said, "Why, if you're not in New York, you are camping out."

URBAN ESCAPES

City living is synonymous with the noise of traffic, with the rush and bustle of commuters, the feel of hard pavements underfoot, the smell of pollution, the crashing sound of machinery on construction sites, the constant ringing of other people's mobile phones, and the inevitable, unwanted listening-in to their conversations.

To be able to turn one's back on all these sounds and smells and be at peace inside the walls that mark the boundaries of one's urban space is a luxury, for not many city houses or apartment buildings have been designed with this in mind. Miraculously, the owners of the urban homes featured here have found that peace. Each has done so by creating a space that honors the human above all else.

These are people who are alive to the buzz and stimulation of city life, who love to visit cafes, cinemas, theaters, and galleries, who require ready access to offices and other people, yet, when their rushing around is done, desire the time and space to dream.

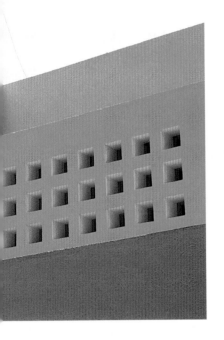

The inspired owners of the Paris apartment have achieved their peace by rising high above that famous European capital city. From their unusual rooftop terrace they can look down on the scurrying urban life below and across to the Eiffel Tower—and all while they have a shower! The French-born interior designer who has returned to his North African roots has swapped the hectic life of Paris and London for the very different urban life of Tangier. His house, overlooking a cemetery on the one side and Tangier harbor on the other, and nestled behind a small, unassuming doorway and thick walls, is his sanctuary. Walls play their part on the outskirts of Mexico City, too, where one visionary architect has built himself a home whose tall concrete walls provide a highly visible barrier against the cacophony of that capital city. Occasional vistas of trees and green spaces belie the fact that the house stands in a residential suburb. In Los Angeles, another farsighted architect has found a very different way to create an oasis of peace in an urban environment. For him the solution has been to build a steel and concrete lookout perched above the city and with an enormous sheltering wall of glass for its owners to hide behind.

When you enter each of these homes, the harried, frenetic pace of urban life slows down. The overwhelming sense of the busy world outside fades and dissolves; tension releases its fierce grip, and a feeling of balance is gradually restored to the soul. The city may be only a step or a bus ride away, but it could just as well be a million miles.

Part of the inspiration for this house in the hills in a western suburb of Mexico City comes from Mediterranean and Islamic architecture—both styles where the harsh and unrelenting sun makes particular demands on the architect. While providing a totally modern solution to the intemperate climate and the rigors of city living, the house's roots in pre-Columbian architecture give it a timeless feel. Surrounded by high walls, which occasionally reveal vistas of trees and green spaces, the house provides an amazing escape from Mexico City. This escape is epitomized by the high-sided corridor that leads from the rusted steel front door to the first courtyard, with its massive concrete steps.

HOTHOUSE URBAN FORTRESS

High protective walls encircle this escape from the urban sprawl of Mexico City. Despite its bold colors and the occasional glimpse of trees and ravines, this is a house that turns in on itself and the earth.

If the architect who designed this dramatic retreat in Las Lomas, in the hills west of Mexico City, were asked who or what was the source of its inspiration, his answer would be, the great Mexican architect, Luis Barragán. When, in 1980, Barragán won architecture's equivalent to the Nobel Prize, he stated his ideal for modern architecture. Buildings were, he said, to have a sense of serenity, mystery, silence, privacy, and the power to astonish. For good measure, he also added sorcery and enchantment.

When its architect-owner demolished his old house in order to build this new one, he followed

The architect-owner is constantly aware of his Mexican heritage and the modern architectural movement. His treatment of color in such a minimalist structure—Mexicans are renowned for their love of color—is subtle. The house was constructed using traditional red-clay bricks covered in a cement-and-gravel render and painted over with specially mixed paints. The colors really come into their own in the courtyard, which plays a central role in the life of the house. Here each plane of the pink-toned walls shades from yellow to orange, to peach, to tangerine, as the sun moves around. The courtyard is stepped like a pre-Columbian temple, with its steps—concealing a garage— planted with *magueyes* or tropical agaves. The courtyard is paved with local volcanic pebbles, while massive early bronze pots point the way to the stone door that leads into the house.

ANY WORK OF ARCHITECTURE WHICH DOES NOT EXPRESS SERENITY IS A MISTAKE. THAT IS WHY IT HAS BEEN AN ERROR TO REPLACE THE PROTECTION OF WALLS WITH TODAY'S INTEMPERATE USE OF ENORMOUS GLASS WINDOWS

Barragán's principles to the letter. The result is a place truly imbued with serenity, mystery, and enchantment. As you approach it from the outside world and again, walking through its rooms and spaces, some of them carved out of the earth and clinging on below ground level, you are filled with a sense of gradual revelation. It is as though the house were reluctant to reveal its true nature except to the few permitted to enter its innermost, most intimate recesses. It is a building that Barragán would surely have described as "an architectural striptease."

The "striptease" starts as soon as you approach. Surrounded by high, protective walls, the house is completely cut off and self-contained, though a hint of trees, barely glimpsed over the walls, gives a tempting illusion of countryside. To add to the

sense of isolation, two steep ravines, one on each side of the house, form an unbreachable barrier between the family that lives here and the roaring urban life that carries on unceasingly outside the walls.

Once you are through the huge rusted steel door, a narrow, high-sided corridor leads to the stepped inner courtyard whose proportions make one feel the real insignificance of human life. From here, another massive, this time stone, door leads to a curved upper reception area, cleverly lit by an opening let into the top of the wall. The many curves that are one hallmark of the work of this owner-architect give the building a calming, human touch.

From the foyer, a descending staircase, lit by a concrete lattice skylight, leads to a service area and offices; then a second staircase takes the visitor on down deeper into the earth to a vestibule, and to the living areas—sitting, dining, library (the most-used part of the house), and bedrooms and bathrooms. At this level, many of the rooms surrounding the inner courtyard open onto it, their large glass windows sliding back for ease of access.

The house is fiercely minimalist in design and concept, but it could never be accused of lacking a heart. Its owner-architect has devised a place to live that is devoid of excess, not in order to depersonalize it, but to provide himself and his family with space to relax and breathe. It gives them what many of us need—"time to stand and stare." No doubt Barragán would approve.

MY HOUSE IS MY REFUGE, AN EMOTIONAL PIECE OF ARCHITECTURE, NOT A COLD PIECE OF CONVENIENCE

THIS PAGE AND OPPOSITE
The owner plays subtle games with light and color, repeating exterior hues on interior walls. Above the staircase leading down to the main living area, a skylight is covered with a yellow concrete lattice. The result—ever-changing patterns.
BELOW Many of the rooms surrounding the inner courtyard open onto it. Squares of local volcanic stone on the terrace are divided by bands of white marble, an effect that is mirrored by the large window. The ancient pots originally carried olive oil from Spain to Mexico.

OPPOSITE, FAR RIGHT, FROM TOP TO BOTTOM
A monolithic dark stone door leads into the curved upper hall paved with a white stone relief-patterned floor. Light floods in from an opening where wall and ceiling meet. A corridor-staircase leads down to the master bedroom and bathroom. Here, a ceiling made of spaced concrete tubes lets light enter and play on the walls. In the master bedroom, a yellow wall and sofa sing out against the neutral colors and natural wood tones. Stone, circular shapes, and the color yellow pick up themes used elsewhere in the house.

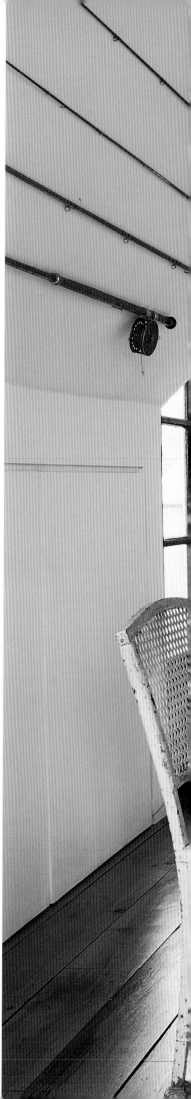

AERIAL VIEWS OF PARIS

High above the rooftops of Paris, this airy eyrie gives a bird's-eye view of the city's landmarks. The bustle below dissolves into a distant murmur.

The old wooden swing in this rooftop apartment says it all. We are obviously in the home of people who dream of freedom—freedom from the confines of the city, freedom to be themselves, freedom to be children again.

The owner of the apartment, with its breathtaking views over Paris, had always wanted a swing like the one at her childhood home in County Cork in Ireland. But she wanted one *inside* her house. And she got it, here in the

ABOVE **At one end of the open-plan salon, armchairs and a sofa inhabit the living area. The wooden floor consists of planks bought in London and salvaged from train cars. To the left, a large painted chest of drawers was rescued from a construction site in Ireland, and above it hangs a collection of fishing rods.**
RIGHT **A massive antique French table and junk-shop chairs make an unusual combination. Stairs in the corner lead to the roof.**

OPPOSITE **The kitchen, with its glass-block ceiling, is regularly flooded with light, while the swing, like so much else here, is recycled—fashioned from pieces of parquet left over from the floor. The mellow wood of the kitchen cabinets comes from a church in Ireland; the tiles are Belgian, while the wall is decorated with German caricatures dating from World War 1.**
LEFT **A beautiful antique bed with wicker panels dominates one of the bedrooms.**

ABOVE **Protected from the elements by a glass conservatory, visitors can enjoy views over Paris from the comfort of this colorful seating.**
LEFT **The inspired rooftop shower makes bathing an invigorating experience. The parapet wall is clothed** in zinc, and the floor of the shower is the glass-block ceiling of the kitchen.
BELOW **Showering on a cold day is a more modest, indoor affair. Decoration is at a minimum and, as elsewhere in the apartment, light floods in from all sides.**

kitchen of this eyrie in the heart of Paris. We are near the Gare du Nord—and only five minutes' walk from the Paris Opéra.

Paris itself was a completely random choice. A few years before, one May, the Irish expatriate had come back to her London home from traveling in China and had found snow. Shortly afterward she went to Paris for a weekend and saw that the sun was shining. She never returned.

The apartment, now with four bedrooms, kitchen-salon, and rooftop terrace featuring an open-air shower, had thirteen rooms when she discovered it three years ago. Pigeons nested in the airy space. The wind whistled through broken tiles in the roof. Now it is a comfortable home—a tribute to the power of the imagination, to ingenuity, and to sound common sense.

For her—painter, photographer, and interior decorator—and her architect and photographer husband, light was the most important factor. So, in no time at all, three extra windows were introduced into what was the servants' quarters of a 1930s building, and a glass-block ceiling was installed above the kitchen. Ingeniously, it doubles as the floor of the roof-top shower. Not a single drop of water has ever dared to seep through to the kitchen.

The roof gives them the ultimate escape, from the concrete jungle and from the busy-ness of life. From here they have a picture-postcard view of Paris, and the Eiffel Tower is reflected in mirrors. With every shower of rain, the colors change. With every shift of light, Paris itself appears to change.

IF YOU ARE LUCKY ENOUGH TO HAVE LIVED IN PARIS AS A YOUNG MAN, THEN WHEREVER YOU GO FOR THE REST OF YOUR LIFE, IT STAYS WITH YOU, FOR PARIS IS A MOVEABLE FEAST

For the French-born interior designer to escape from the life he lives in London and Paris, he needs to immerse himself in another culture, "to breathe another land." This house, next to a Muslim cemetery and with glimpses of the Atlas Mountains, leaves European culture far behind.

RECOLLECTIONS OF TANGIER

Friday is the favorite day of the week for the French-born interior designer who is the fortunate owner of this calm city refuge in Tangier.

For Friday is holy day, the day when the simple Muslim cemetery next door springs into life and color, and fills with mourning families who come to eat, drink, and pray from daybreak to dusk amid the sound of sheep's bells and shepherds' chidings echoing in from the surrounding hills. These are people who calmly accept that death is an inevitable part of life, whose children do not fear to play among the tombstones of their ancestors.

It was his roots that led the Frenchman to the house with the cemetery on one side and the Atlantic on the other. His artist-grandfather before him had come to North Africa, and it was there that his beautiful wife died, tragically young. In the next generation, the owner's mother was brought up in

To stand on the roof terrace of this old house west of Tangier is to understand its special magic. From here there are views of mountains to the east, Tangier Bay, a distant Gibraltar and Spain to the north and, on three sides, the simple Muslim cemetery. The terrace, with its restful atmosphere despite the fact that the house stands in the middle of town, is a place to read, sleep, drink mint tea, or dine. There are simple terracotta tiles underfoot; a large yellow-painted wall is home to a lush bougainvillea; cacti grow enthusiastically in pots; and cushioned concrete benches and wicker furniture provide comfortable seating. Traditional touches are the carved wooden tables and pierced metal lanterns.

LEFT This tiled hall opens onto the living area below, bedrooms and bathrooms on the same level, and the roof terrace and sky above. In restoring the house, the owner used local materials and colors. The tiles, wrought-iron banisters, colored glass above the doors, deep red-brown paint of the woodwork, and the whitewash of the walls were all obtained locally.
BELOW The guest bedroom contains an array of fabrics bought in the local kasbah. Their colors and patterns mean this room feels totally Moroccan and not like an oasis of Parisian or London chic transplanted to a foreign land.

HE IS THE HAPPIEST, BE HE KING OR PEASANT, WHO FINDS PEACE IN HIS HOME

Algeria, so this retreat is part of the Frenchman's North African heritage.

Though he could have chosen to live in Tangier's kasbah, the French-born designer preferred the more open aspect of Tangier Bay, with views of both Gibraltar and Spain. Tangier, which earlier in the twentieth century had been one of the most stylish resorts in the Mediterranean, has proved an endless source of inspiration for him. In the town itself, he discovered the secret, interlocked life of narrow shaded twisting lanes, opulent houses hiding

OPPOSITE, ABOVE AND LEFT The master bedroom and its bathroom take up half of the second floor. Locally made fabrics decorate the walls and furniture, and a bold flatweave rug softens the tiled floor. An unusual touch is the English-made Poole pottery vase on the beaten copper table.
OPPOSITE, BELOW On the terrace there is a cool sleeping platform. All the fabrics here, including the Ethiopian umbrella, were bought in the souk. The skylight above the upstairs hall can be seen on the right of the sleeping area.

behind blank facades, and the feeling of endless humming activity that an artist can never tire of exploring. And the surrounding countryside is magnificent, too—unspoiled, unchanged, and redolent with a sense of biblical times.

The Frenchman's neighbors are the ordinary, working people of Tangier, living in modest, unpretentious homes, just like his own. It was the innate simplicity of the house that was one of its attractions, and he decided that, whatever the cost, he must preserve that. The house was old, but how old no one could tell, for in this part of the world the centuries leave little mark on the style of building. But the years had added their accretions. To return the timeworn house to something approaching its former self, these had to be removed and its soul restored.

The house is on two floors with a roof terrace that overlooks the cemetery. You approach it off the narrow, dusty street through a small door. Only the protective ironwork grille sets it apart

HOME IS ABOUT THE FAMILIAR, ABOUT GRAVITY, ABOUT FALLING BACK INTO THE SELF AFTER BEING DISPERSED AND OVER-EXTENDED

THIS PAGE **On the ground floor of the house a simple corridor leads from the (uninspiring) front door into a glorious living and dining space, rich with the colors and artefacts of Morocco. The furniture is local to Tangier—some old, some new. The distressed painted chest in the dining area is an old piece from the Palais Scott. This ancient and eccentric local mansion once owned by an Englishman is redolent with personal associations for the house's owner, recalling many of his first experiences of Tangier.**
OPPOSITE **A corner of the living area is furnished with locally made textiles and carved wooden tables of differing periods. The Moorish-style arch is one of several that the owner added to the house.**

from its neighbors. On the ground floor are the kitchen, living and dining areas, and a cool, quiet room for reading and writing, decorated with Moroccan works of art. The second floor consists of the main bedroom area—which comprises a sitting area, bathroom, and dressing

LEFT One of the new arches leads into a quiet room for reading or writing, which remains delightfully cool in the heat of the summer. Here, local weaving intended for a mosque adorns the lower part of the wall. The photographs above are mainly of Morocco in the early years of the century. Many depict the owner's grandfather aboard his yacht, wearing the robes of the Bedouin of southern Morocco. RIGHT Shut away from the surrounding streets and ornately decorated parts of the kasbah, the modest house is the epitome of domestic Moroccan architectural design, with its blank walls concealing hidden riches. Only the simple ironwork grille and the pair of mosaic pots indicate that the owner is not one of the locals.

"NYUMBA NJEMA SI MLANGO" A GOOD HOUSE IS NOT JUDGED BY ITS DOOR.

room—while on the other side of the hall is the guest bedroom with a second bathroom.

Follow a small staircase up from this hall and you emerge, facing the cemetery, into the blinding sunlight of the roof terrace. Here, a canvas awning shades one side of the terrace, fat plump cushions soften concrete benches, wicker furniture offers itself up to your contours, and a cool white-painted, curtained-off room with a soft mattress beckons you to sleep.

In restoring the house, the owner preserved all possible features, adding only those in keeping with this style of modest Moroccan home. All the furniture, fabrics, textiles, and decorative items were picked up in flea markets or the souk, and it was in the souk that he found the earth pigments—the yellows, red-browns, and ochers that are at the heart of Moroccan art and design, and which form the basis for his paint colors.

And now, on his many visits to his secluded house beside the cemetery, the French interior designer has found the change he was longing for, the inspiration needed to fire his artistic imagination, and the style of life that complements but does not replace his life in London and Paris.

Perched in the Hollywood hills high above Los Angeles, this architect-designed steel, glass, and concrete home basks in its urban setting.

LOS ANGELES LOOKOUT

The moment architect Brian Murphy's clients turned the steep corner of the winding track and saw the small promontory in Outpost Canyon high above Los Angeles in the Hollywood Hills, they fell in love with it. They knew this

was a place where they could escape from the stresses of the Hollywood film world in which they moved and worked. But they didn't fall in love with the nondescript, shambolic 1960s house that stood on the promontory, so down it came. What they wanted was "a home with a kick," and Murphy was the man to give it to them.

Well known for his innovative use of steel, massive expanses of glass, and solid blocks of concrete, Murphy has created, on the footings of the

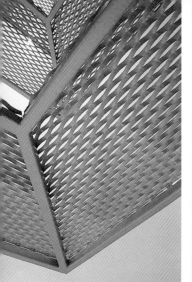

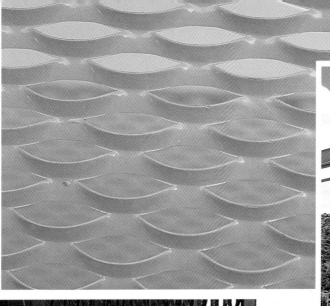

old house, a home that is a thoroughly modern expression of human domination of structure and materials. Its *raison d'être* is the magnificent site itself and the views it encompasses, hence its sweeping elliptical roof sheltering walls of windows that look out over the vast, sprawling city of Los Angeles below. This dramatic, unafraid roof dips and rises to make the most of the striking views and, where necessary, to shield its occupants from the eyes of their neighbors.

The brief Murphy's clients gave him was to provide them with a home where they could indulge their passion for entertaining, but where they could also enjoy their privacy. They must be well pleased with the results. On the ground floor stands a wide-open space—ideal for entertaining—broken up only by the kitchen and bar. One area flows seamlessly into the next, and the beautiful swimming pool is just a step away, sheltered from the blazing California sun by the overhanging roof and a multitude of balconies.

That idiosyncratic roof supports a mezzanine level that cleverly provides the owners with a

OPPOSITE **The specially designed expanded metal awnings wrap themselves around the house, protecting the interior from the strong summer sun and creating patterns of dappled light and shade. The 8-foot- (2.5 meter) high sliding glass doors between the main living area and the pool terrace were custom made. They allow the side of the house to be opened to the elements.**

RIGHT **Los Angeles spreads itself out 1,000 feet (300 meters) below the house. Just to the left of this balcony are breathtaking views over the canyon.**

ABOVE **The massive glass front door set in a wall of glass leads from the yard into the house. Nothing stands in the way of the view right through from the front to the back of the house. To enhance this feeling of unencumbered space, furnishings are kept to a minimum—just a few favorite antiques and a much-used piano.**

IN CALIFORNIA … NOBLE MOUNTAINS, LOVELY LITTLE HILLS AND CANYONS … HOLD THE RECORD OF THIS GENERATION'S HISTORY, IDEALS, SENSE OF ROMANCE …

useful secondary public space, an area where they and their guests can watch television without disrupting the rest of the house and its activities.

The private spaces—the master bedroom with its two bathrooms, the office, and the guest accommodation – are tucked away at the back of the house, completely secluded from the sometimes thronged public areas.

Murphy has created a contemporary design that truly rejoices in itself and its boldness, where even the swimming pool has been deliberately positioned to provide a reflection of the house's structure. And yet it also manages to be a design that embraces its surroundings. From wherever you look out, its stark concrete and rolled-steel elements frame the views of the city beyond and of the wooded canyon below. There can be no doubt that this is a house that belies the assertion of detective-story writer Raymond Chandler, that Los Angeles is a "big hard-boiled city with no more personality than a paper cup."

BELOW **The kitchen and bar, with their custom-built cabinets, introduce an element of color into the otherwise white and gray interior. Brushed stainless steel base units and work surfaces set off the red lacquer finish of the wall cabinets and the blue seats of the stools. The windows afford views of the hills and the city.**

SOURCES OF QUOTATIONS

INTRODUCTION

10
"You do not need to leave your room
... remain ... at your table and listen.
Do not even listen, simply wait. Do not
even wait, be quite still and solitary. The
world will freely offer itself to you."
Franz Kafka (1883–1924)

13
"Live with the gods. And he does so
who constantly shows them that his
soul is satisfied with what is assigned
to him."
Marcus Aurelius (121–80 B.C.)

14
"When from our better selves we have
too long been parted by the hurrying
world, and droop, sick of its business, of
its pleasures tired, how gracious, how
benign is solitude."
William Wordsworth (1770–1850)
The Prelude

16
"Building upon the land is as natural to
man as to other animals, birds or
insects."
Frank Lloyd Wright (1869–1959)
Architecture and Modern Life

RURAL ESCAPES

THE CROOKED HOUSE

23
"The vernacular housing stock of Wales
is being impoverished in the name of
restoration. I believe in buildings
retaining their time-worn shape."
Marc Swan (owner) to Judith Miller

24
"The charm, attraction, character, call it
what you will, of the house is that it
has grown over the years in a
haphazard sort of way."
The Duchess of Devonshire
The House: Portrait of Chatsworth
Copyright Macmillan 1982

MOROCCAN CHIAROSCURO

30
"In violent and chaotic times ... our
only chance for survival lies in creating
our own little islands of sanity and
order, in making havens of our homes."
Sue Kaufman
Falling Bodies

33
"A house is no home unless it contain
food and fire for the mind as well as
for the body."
Margaret Fuller
Woman in the Nineteenth Century

34
"This house is not a vision of
architecture, but ... the taking of an ...
old form and adding ... to create a
cosy ... retreat."
Elie Mouyal (owner) to Judith Miller

TIMELESS RURAL IDYLL

36
"This was what I prayed for: a plot of
land not too large, containing a garden,
and near the house, a fresh spring of
water and a bit of forest to complete
it."
Horace (65–8 B.C.)
Satires

WATERSIDE ESCAPES

BOATHOUSE BELLE

45
"Now the great winds shoreward blow,
Now the salt tides seawards flow;
Now the wild white horses play,
Champ and chafe and toss in the
spray."
Matthew Arnold (1822–1888)
The Forsaken Merman

46
"There is nothing ... half so much
worth doing as simply messing about
in boats."
Kenneth Grahame (1859–1932)
The Wind in the Willows
Copyright The University Chest,
Oxford, reproduced by permission of
Curtis Brown, London

MINIMAL IN MALIBU

51
"If you want a golden rule that will fit
everybody, this is it: have nothing in
your houses that you do not know to
be useful, or believe to be beautiful."
William Morris (1834–96)
Hopes and Fears for Art

53
"In all circumstances, however hard
they may be, we should rejoice rather
than be cast down, that we may not
lose the greatest good, the peace and
tranquility of our soul."
Attrib. St. John of the Cross
(1542–1591)

MEXICAN COASTAL JUNGLE
RETREAT

58
"The voice of the sea speaks to the
soul. The touch of the sea is sensuous,
enfolding the body in its soft, close
embrace."
Kate Chopin (1851–1904)
The Awakening

61
"There is a pleasure in the pathless
woods,
There is a rapture on the lonely shore,
There is society, where none intrudes,
By the deep sea, and music in its roar:
I love not man the less, but nature
more."
Lord Byron (1788–1824)
The Childe Harold"s Pilgrimage

ATLANTIC BASTION

70
"They that go down to the sea in ships,
and occupy their business in great
waters, these see the works of the lord
and his wonders in the deep."
The Bible, Psalm 107

BLUE OCEAN-LAPPED
PARADISE

81
"I was set free! I dissolved in the sea,
became white sails and flying spray,
became beauty and rhythm, became
moonlight and the ship and the high
dim-starred sky. I belonged, without
past or future within peace and unity
and a wild joy."
Eugene O'Neill (1888–1953)
Long Day's Journey into Night
Copyright Yale University Press

82
"Blue colour is everlastingly appointed
by the deity to be a source of delight."
John Ruskin (1819–1900)

MOUNTAIN & HILLSIDE
ESCAPES

STAIRWAY TO HEAVEN

90
"There is a silence into which the world
cannot intrude. There is an ancient
peace you carry in your heart."
A Course in Miracles

92
"We need time to dream, time to
remember, and time to reach the
infinite. Time to be."
Gladys Taber

95
"No person who is not a great sculptor
or painter can be an architect. if he is
not a sculptor or painter, he can only
be a builder."
John Ruskin (1819–1900)

IN THE MANDRASCATE
MANNER

98
"All real and wholesome enjoyments
possible to man ... to watch the corn
grow, and the blossoms set; to draw
hard breath over ploughshare or
spade; to read, to think, to love, to
hope, to pray—these are the things
that make men happy."
John Ruskin (1819–1900)

100
"The house ... is his castle and
fortress, as well for his defence against
injury ... as for his repose."
Sir Edward Coke (1552–1634)

WILD ADVENTURES IN THE
ADIRONDACKS

104
"Over all the mountaintops is peace ...
birds in the forest are silent ... soon,
you, too, will have peace."
J. W. von Goethe (1749–1832)
Wanderers Nachtlied

106
"A man must keep a little back shop
where he can be himself without
reserve. In solitude alone can he know
true freedom."
Michel de Montaigne (1533–92)
Essays

109
"The country habit has me by the
heart,
For he's bewitched forever who has
seen.
Not with his eyes but with his vision,
Spring flow down the woods and
stipple leaves with sun"
Vita Sackville-West (1892–1962)
Copyright, the Estate of Vita Sackville-
West, reproduced by permission of
Curtis Brown, London

MOUNTAIN RESCUE

112
"Well! some people talk of morality,
and some of religion, but give me a
snug little property."
Maria Edgeworth (1767–1849)
The Absentee

ACKNOWLEDGMENTS

I would like to thank Simon Upton for his wonderful photography and Eithne Power for her substantial contribution to the text. I would also like to thank the team at Ryland, Peters & Small for all their skills, dedication and patience: Paul Tilby for the design and layout, Hilary Mandleberg for editing; Tessa Thornley for editorial assistance, Kate Brunt and Sarah Hepworth for location research and Meryl Silbert for production control.

Together with the publisher, I would also like to offer heartfelt thanks to the following homeowners, architects and designers for allowing us to photograph their homes and/or work. JM

Gretchen Bellinger

Burt Berdis and Sherry Spees

Lucio and Luisa Bonaccorsi

Ann Boyd

John Burningham and Helen Oxenbury

Jennifer Castle

Jeffrey Cayle

Alexandra Champalimaud

Charles Chauliaguet

Jo Crepain

Françoise Dorget

Kate Earle and Emily Todhunter

Sarah Featherstone

François Gilles

June Hilton

Karen Howes

Anthony Hudson

Pamela Ludwig

Christine Madsen

Jan Moereels

Karsten and Barbara Moller

Ian Morrison

Elie Mouyal

Brian Murphy

Sue Nye and Gavin Davies

Lynne and Patrick Palanza

Tatjana Patitz

Ana P. Pous

Guiseppe Prato

J. Morgan Puett and Mark Dion

Frank and Trish Purcel

Ricardo Regazzoni and Guido Stockman

Carol Reid and Jean-François Galliard

Dot Spikings

Scott Sternberg and Nicki Huggins

Mark and Tia Swan

Mr and Mrs François Von Hurter

Ann Young

Jose Yturbe

Architects and designers whose work is featured in this book:

BAM Construction/Design Inc.
Brian Alfred Murphy
Architect
150 W. Channel Road
Santa Monica
CA 90402
USA
t. 310 459 0955
Pages: 118–121, 164–165, 186–189

Barefoot Elegance
Dot Spikings and Jennifer Castle
3537 Old Coneyo Road
Suite 105
Newbury Park
CA 91320
USA
t. 805 499 5959
Pages: 11, 40–41, 48–55

Gretchen Bellinger Inc.
Textile Designer and Owner of Camp Bellinger
Post Office Box 64
31 Ontario Street
Cohoes
NY 12047
USA
t. 518 235 2828
f. 518 235 4242
e-mail gretchenbellinger@juno.com
Pages: 9 (inset–center), 15BR, 85 (inset–left), 87 (inset–right), 102–109

Ann Boyd Design Ltd.
33 Elystan Street
London SW3 3NT
England
t. + 44 20 7591 0202
Pages: 36–39

Jeffrey Cayle
Designer
69 Horatio Street
Third Floor
New York
NY 10014
USA
Pages: 142–147

Charles Chauliguet
Architect
Contact through Caravane as below
Pages: 76–83

Alexandra Champalimaud and Associates Inc.
Interior Architecture and Design
One Union Square West, Suite 603
New York
NY 10003
USA
t. 212 807 8869
f. 212 807 1742
www.acainteriordesign.com
Pages: 130 (inset–centre), 148–153

Jo Crepain
Architect
Vlaandernstraat 6
8-2000 Antwerp
Belgium
t. + 32 3 213 61 61
www.jocrepain.com
Pages: 130 (inset–right), 134–141

Françoise Dorget
Interior Designer
Caravane
6 rue Pavée
75004 Paris
France
t. + 33 1 44 61 04 20
f. + 33 1 44 61 04 22
Pages: 76–83

Featherstone Associates
Sarah Featherstone
74 Clerkenwell Road
London EC1M 5QA
England
t. + 44 20 7490 1212
f. + 44 20 7490 1313
sarah.f@featherstone-associates.co.uk
www.featherstone-associates.co.uk
Pages: 8–9, 40 (inset–right), 42–43TL, 68–75

Hudson Architects
Anthony Hudson
49–59 Old Street
London EC1V 9HX
England
t. + 44 20 7490 3411
f. + 44 20 7490 3412
anthonyh@hudsonarchitects.co.uk
www.hudsonarchitects.co.uk
Pages: 8–9, 40 (inset–right), 42–43TL, 68–75

IPL Interiors
François Gilles and Dominque Lubar
25 Bullen Street
Battersea
London SW11 3ER
England
t. + 44 20 7978 4224
f. + 44 20 7978 4334
Pages: endpapers, 6, 7, 166C, 178–185

J. Morgan Puett
www.jmorganpuett.com
Pages: 130–131, 130 (inset–left), 154–163, 190–191

Elie Mouyal
Architect
Rue Saâd Bnou Oubada n° 336 ISSIL
Boîte Postale N° 3667 Amerchich
Marrakech
Morocco
t. + 212 4 30 05 02
Pages: 1, 18 (inset–right), 20 (inset–left, right), 28–35

Tia Swan
Bed and Breakfast
Crooked House
P.O. Box 13
Knighton DO
LD8 2WE
England
Pages: 18 (inset–left, center), 18–19, 20 (inset–center), 21A, 22–27

Guiseppe Prato
Architect
t. + 39 95 375 261
Pages: 96–101

Todhunter Earle Interiors
Chelsea Reach
1st Floor
79–89 Lots Road
London SW10 0RN
England
t. + 44 20 7349 9999
www.todhunterearle.com
Pages: 4–5, 110–117

José de Yturbe
De Yturbe Arquitectos
Patriotismo 13 (4° piso)
Lomas de Barrilaco
Mexico 11010 DF
t. + 525 540 368
f. + 525 520 8621
e-mail deyturbe@infosel.net.mx
Pages: 2–3, 17BR, 43C, 56–63, 166–167TL&TR, 167BR, 168–173